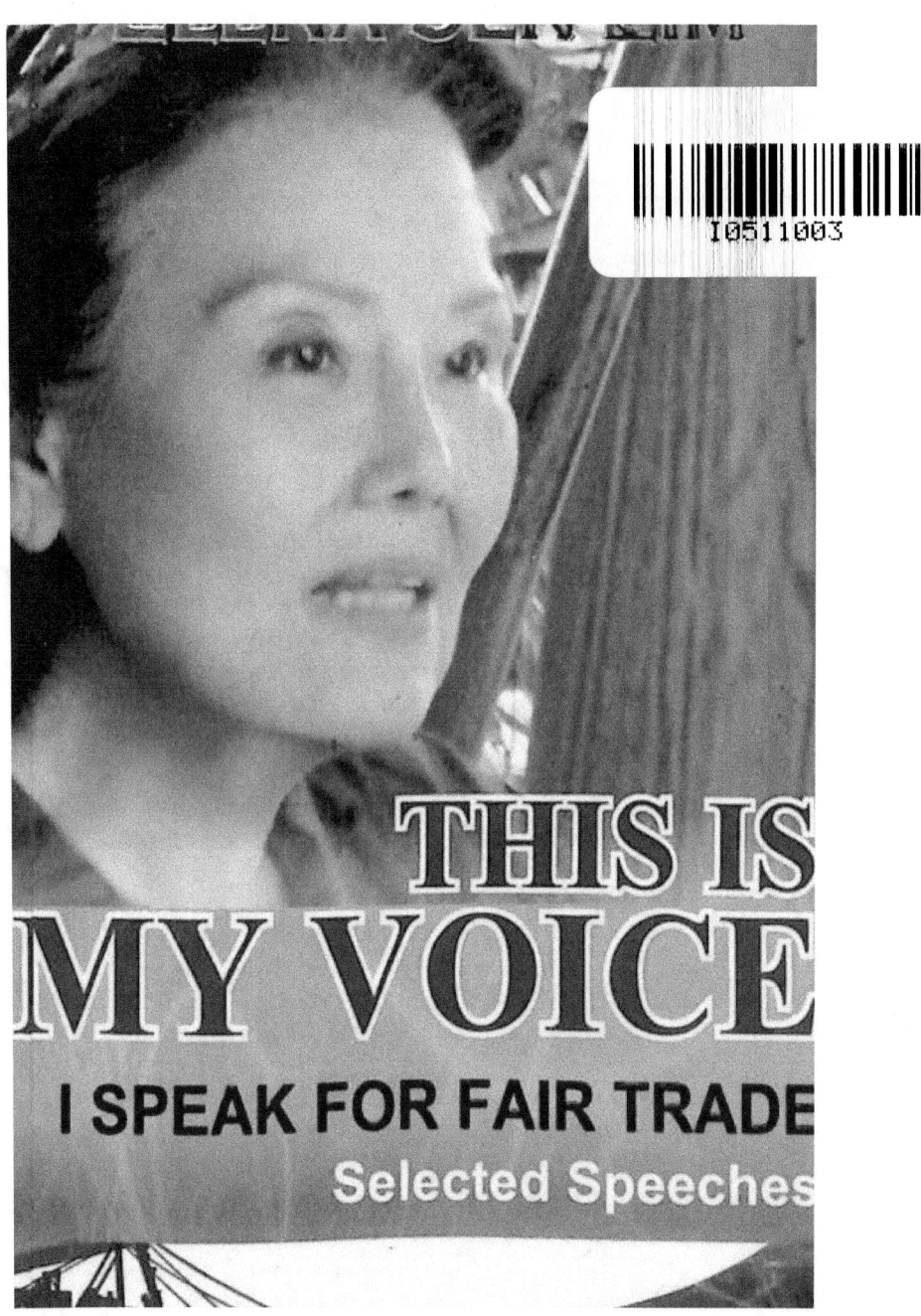

THIS IS MY VOICE

I SPEAK FOR FAIR TRADE

Selected Speeches

Elena Sen Lim

*Published and reprinted in 2017 in USA by
TATAY JOBO ELIZES. Self-Publisher, under the
permission and authorization of the author, ELENA SEN
LIM, who owns the copyright to this book. The Author can
withdraw this permission at her discretion without any
objection from Talay Jobo Elizes at any time. Printing of
this book is using the present day method of Print-On-
Demand (POD) system, where prints will never run out of
copies to be available for posterity. The copyright owner
is free to republish with other publishers
and printers anytime.*

*ISBN - 13: 978 - 1548321512
ISBN - 10: 1548321516*

To my children:
Susan,
David,
Jason,
Vincent

My grandchildren:
Kevin,
CJ,
Isabel,
JJ,
Melissa,
Michelle,
Jemboy,
Michael,
Marvin,
Matthew,
Meggy,
Anika

Find your voice.

ACKNOWLEDGMENTS

I humbly thank the many institutions — schools, civic clubs, local and foreign organizations — which have given me the honor and opportunity to speak before their leaders and members. From them, I have learned much. I treasure the lessons learned as gems in my life's journey. Priceless gems of their kindness and generosity.

Likewise, my deepest appreciation and gratitude to two friends I cherish and respect — **Senator Sergio "Serge" R. Osmena** III and popular columnist **Hilarion "Larry" M. Henares, Jr.** -- for their kind words in the Foreword and Afterword they did, respectively.

As can be gleaned from their brief profiles which I have included in this book, Serge and Larry are both men of great intellect, integrity, courage, and patriotism. They have devoted most of their lives to serving our beloved Filipino nation and, for me, it is a priceless honor to be considered their friend.

My heartfelt thanks, too, to my friends who helped me put this book together: Raymond L. Toledo, Editorial Consultant and photographer (cover photo); Haydee P. Toledo, Associate Editorial Consultant; Domingo Cortez, Cover Designer; and Viktor P. Toledo, Art Consultant.

FOREWORD
by Senator Sergio R. Osmeha III

Outspoken is a definite understatement to describe Elena Lim.

Long recognized and respected as one of the Philippines ' most successful entrepreneurs, Ms. Lim minces no words whenever she is asked to speak before varied groups whether in the Philippines or abroad.

Her speeches are delivered with such boldness and candor that are refreshing and thought provoking. Her many daring and fearless opposition to many policies and laws have more often than not caused policymakers to undertake a review of such policies.

Elena has always possessed an uncanny ability to think outside of the box. The exquisite timing of her business ventures have been superb, from the pioneering assembly of SONY television sets to her venture into international shrimp processing and trading to her successful positioning of "MyPhone" in an already overcrowded telecommunications market. Her fearless attempts to tilt at windmills such as the liberalization of international trade which has placed domestic firms at the mercy of vast, interlocking, well- funded foreign business combines have earned for Elena the admiration and respect of her peers not only in local business federations but even from members of powerful foreign business councils like the KEIDANREN of Japan.

Elena's speeches in this book contain dozens of her significant ideas, opinions and proposals. It is an eminently entertaining and informative read and would make excellent reference material for en-trepreneurs, economists, business analysts and students of economic history. It is a seminal contribution to the continually evolving story of a developing country's travails in adjusting to the new rules of transnational trade.

The Philippines is certainly better off because she has produced multi-talented and productive citizens such as Elena Lim.

Profile of Senator Sergio R. Osmena III

(source: www.senate.gov.ph)

Tagged as the Senate's "Maverick" for being fiercely independent, Senator Serge Osmena, who is of Cebuano-Negrense-Ilonggo ancestry, takes pride that his family has had the honor to have contributed three generations of direct descendants to serve in the Philippine Senate. Both his grandfathers - Sergio Osmena Sr. and Esteban dela Rama - and his father, Sergio Osmena Jr., had been prominent lawmakers.

He has pursued the enactment into law of 183 bills, such as the Absentee Voting Law, Retail Trade Liberalization Act, Government Procurement Act, Securities Regulations Code, and the Regional Headquarters for Multi-National Companies Act, and of which he co-authored 55, including the Agriculture and Fisheries Modernization Act, the Clean Air Act, the Anti-Money Laundering Act and the Safeguards Measures Act. He is currently the chairman, of the Committee on Banks, Financial Institu- tions and Currencies and the Committee on Energy. He has been elected chairman of the Joint Congressional Power Commission.

Among the bills that he seeks approval of during the 15th Congress are the Freedom of Information Act, the Fair Trade Act, the amendments to the Anti-Money Laundering law, the Insurance Code and the Bangko Sentral Charter.

In keeping with his family's heritage, the senator has dedicated his legislative effort to bringing down the cost of doing business in the Philippines in order to encourage private enterprises to create more jobs for Filipinos. He has always emphasized the development of the countryside where the poorest of the poor live. Out of his total 3,251 infrastructure projects in all 79 provinces, 80% were constructed in the rural areas.

A firm believer that education is the great equalizer, Senator Osmena has championed the fundamental need of all Filj- pino children to be properly trained to meet the challenges of life. He has funded a total of 935 school buildings all over the country. The senator has likewise directed sub stantial budgetary support to government- owned medical institutions to fund the medical needs of indigent patients. To date, a total 6f 11,883 Filipinos have been the beneficiaries of Sen. Osmena's medical assistance program at the Philippine General Hospital (PGH), National Kidney Institute (NKI), the Philippine Heart Center (PHC) the Lung Center of the

Philippines, the East Avenue Medical Center, and the Baguio General Hospital.

Senator Osmena has earned the reputation of being the Senate's fearless fighter against corruption. His numerous exposes on graft and corruption, among others the anomalous SSS-EPCI bank sale, IMPSA- CBK, PIATCO, Tiwi-Makban, Marconi radar and Casecnan power contracts, have saved billions of pesos for the Filipino people.

Senator Serge Osmena is a farmer and businessman by training and was educated at Harvard, Georgetown, and the University of the Philippines. He is married to Bet- tina Mejia Lopez of Iloilo, Pampanga, and Leyte and has six children.

POSTSCRIPT:

I must add to this official profile of Senator Serge Osmena a personal note: As far as Fm concerned' he is the most brilliant, dedicated, and productive senator /public servant I have ever known.

He is also a very kind man. I personally know of unpublicized acts of kindness he has extended to small Filipinos, with no strings attached. It's small acts of kindness from his heart.

What many young Filipinos, born long after Martial Law, may not know about Senator Osmena is that parts of his life are the stuff of legend.

He was arrested by the soldiers of former President Ferdinand Marcos right after the declaration of Martial Law on September 21, 1972.

After five years (1972-1977) of imprisonment as a political detainee of the Marcos Dictatorship, he and his cellmate, the late Geny Lopez, former Chairman of ABS-CBN Broadcasting Corporation, made a daring escape from their maximum-security prison in Fort Bonifacio.

After a long, arduous, and dangerous process, they were able to dig a tunnel from their cell to a spot outside the camp s perimeter.

There, a car waited for them which spirited them out to a small airport in Dagupan, Pangasinan, from where they took a small plane to Hong Kong, thence to the United States of America where they sought political asylum.

This historic exploit was later immortalized in the movie "Eskapo" featuring big Filipino stars like Richard Gomez.

In the U.S. he continued his involvement in the anti-Marcos Dictatorship struggle by serving as the director for Movement for a Free Philippines.

Right after the assassination of former Senator Benigno "Ninoy" Aquino on August 21, 1983, he became the founding director of JAJA or Justice for Aquino, Justice for All movement.

He returned to the Philippines after the 1986 EDSA People Power bloodless revolt which finally ousted the Marcos Dictatorship.

A bit of history for the youth

Allow me to share a bit more about Philippine history, especially for the

*youth of today, and tomorrow. So many Filipinos -young and old alike —
have no sense, no appreciation, of history.*

*They have neither awareness nor understanding of critical historical
events which have resulted in the problems we face today.*

*They forget that there is much truth in the saying that, "Those who
forget the past are condemned to repeat it."*

And so a bit of history:

*Serge is the grandson of former President Sergio Osmena, Sr., and the
son of former Senator Sergio "Serging" Osmena, Jr.; both forebears
exemplified excellence and integrity in public service; both were victims of
political mishaps in their quest for the presidency in 1946 and 1969,
respectively.*

*Sergio Osmena, Sr., was the Vice President of President Manuel L.
Quezon during the early years of World War II.*

*Shortly after Japan invaded the Philippines on December 8, 1941,
President Quezon and Vice President Osmena set up a government in exile
in the United States.*

*When President Quezon died of tuberculosis on August 1, 1944, in New
York, Osmena became President.*

*On the same year, President Osmena accompanied U.S. General
Douglas MacArthur during the landing of U.S. forces in Leyte on October
20, 1944.*

*Upon his arrival, President Osmena found a Filipino nation totally
devastated by war, a conflict not of our making which led to the loss of more
than ONE MILLION Filipino lives.*

*Sometime in 1946, in the ill-timed clamour of Filipino politicians for
independence, the U.S. government immediately granted us independence.*

*Thus, the Americans considered themselves absolved from the
responsibility of rehabilitation and reconstruction of our ravaged land.*

*We became a mere incident or footnote in history, a dispensable
sacrificial lamb in a war not of our own making.*

*A very painful and ironic historical fact must always be remembered by
all Filipinos: The United States government provided much more aid and
resources to help its enemy, Japan, recover after the war, than it did to its
"ally," the Philippines.*

*To add massive insult to massive injury, not only did the U.S.
government give much less aid to the Philippines - in 1946 the U.S.
Congress passed the heinous and infamous "Rescission Act of1946" which
CANCELLED the benefits due all Filipinos victimized by the war, including
the valiant Filipino guerrillas who fought alongside the U.S. forces.*

*The official justification for this supremely treacherous act was that the
U.S. government had allegedly already released 200 million dollars to the
Philippines after the war.*

*The magnitude of this insult is underscored by the fact that out of 66
countries allied with the United States during World War II, only the*

Philippines was denied military benefits! (source: http://en. wikipedia. org/wiki/Rescission_Act_of_1946)

It was only in 2009 - more than 60 years later and after non-stop, desperate lobbying by Filipino veterans' groups and their supporters - that the U.S. Congress provided, under Section 1002 of the American Recovery and Reinvestment Act, a one-time US$15,000 lump sum for the surviving veterans who are US Citizens, and a US$9,000 lump sum settlement for non-citizens.

This is why many critics of the long-delayed compensation allege that the U.S. government deliberately and callously waited for majority of the veterans to die before approving compensation for survivors.

It is no wonder then that many young Filipino activists feverishly join rallies before the U.S. embassy and say, "With friends like the Americans, who needs enemies?"

Pardon the above digression but I just couldn't resist the opportunity to bring to the attention of readers these vital historical facts... especially to young readers who were born long after the Second World War and have no idea of what happened then.

Back to our discussion on President Osmena: In 1946, a national election was held.

As the incumbent, President Osmena. could have easily won any election. But like a true statesman, he remarked, "I will not campaign. The Filipino people know my track record of 40 years of public service. There are far more pressing things to be done. The reconstruction of a ruined country comes before any politics. I will devote my time to start the rebuilding and rehabilitation of all damaged facilities and losses of land and people, which is more urgent than any political ambition."

And so he never campaigned. His time was focused on the healing of the wounds of war, both physically and spiritually.

Thus, the young politician, Manuel Roxas, won that hastily called election, unopposed and aided by the Americans.

In gratitude, Roxas advocated the grant of Parity Rights to the Americans.

President Sergio Osmena, Sr., died in 1961.

Eight years later, in the 1969 presidential election, his son, Senator Sergio Osmena, Jr., ran against the incumbent President Ferdinand Marcos.

The clamor for change, at that time, was feverish. The "OK" ("Osmena Kami") thumbs-up sign was flashed all over the land against the "V" sign for "Victory" of Marcos.

"Serging," as he was fondly called by his followers, longed for a new deal for our Filipino people with focus on the Economy and not on Politics.

He was running on the platform: "Ang Dalubhasang Ekonomista" ("The Expert Economist"). This was not an empty boast. He was a summa cum laude graduate (Bachelor of Science in Commerce) of New York

University in 1938.

Unfortunately, the incumbent Marcos' political machinery (described by many political analysts as the "3 Gs" of Guns, Goons, and Gold) proved too much for the idealistic challenger Osmena. Amidst much controversy; Marcos was declared the winner of the 1969 election.

Then on the evening of August 21, 1971, two grenades were thrown onstage at a political rally of the Liberal Party at Plaza Miranda, Quiapo, Manila. Nine people died and 95 others were severely injured. Serging was among those gravely wounded.

Over the next several years, despite several operations, a number of shrapnel fragments remained embedded in his body because removing them would endanger his life further. As a result, he became too sick to run again for public office.

Along with Senator Osmena, other leaders of the Liberal Party were also critically wounded, such as Senators Jovito Salonga, Eddie Ilarde, and Eva Estrada-Kalaw.

Thus, the Filipino nation for the second time was deprived of a holistic leadership which, under a Sergio Osmena, Jr., could have changed the lives of our people.

His expertise on the economy could have uplifted the lives of majority of the poor. The need of the hour was a man who could focus on the Economy and not on Traditional Politics.

We lost two great moments. Men with the qualities of sterling excellence and integrity who lived lives dedicated to truth and service.

Serging died in 1984. Two years later, his son, Serge Osmena III, would go back to the Philippines from exile in the United States.

Upon his return, he worked as director for various top Philippine corporations.

In 1995, upon the invitation of then President Fidel Ramos to join the Lakas-Laban senatorial slate, he ran and won a Senate seat.

He is now serving another six-year term until 2016, as an Independent.

His record has proven him to be competent, incorruptible, decent and visionary (truly like his father "Dalubhasang Ekonomista, Hindi Pulitiko"). A man of constancy who does not compromise on anything that would diminish the nation's honor and character.

In the boisterous celebration of the Chinese New Year this year, majority of our lawmakers wanted to declare the Chinese New Year as a National Holiday.

Only the lone voice of Senator Serge Osmena prevented its declaration. His rationale was simple. To do so would open the floodgate for the other nations to request a similar privilege and, thus, would make us the laughing-stock of the world with so many holidays. To Senator Osmena it was not the right and moral thing to do.

He does not give in even to requests for easing his objection to the approval of the appointments of some candidates with the Commission on

Appointments; not even the silent whisper of the highest official of the land can dissuade him when he deemed it not fit and right for the country.

The three generations of Osmenas are not in the category of political dynasties. Each generation had to earn its political victory based on clean records. The right to run for office is not bequeathed or inherited or handed down by sheer power or political connection.

In coming elections, how will the Filipinos vote? By name recall? By the power and influence of older lineage? By political expediency? Or worst, by fraud and deceit? I hope none of these.

Pause. Take to heart the depth of character and knowledge, competence, and track record of the candidate. This is the right test.

Our nation's future lies in our hands, hearts, and minds. We must choose only the most worthy candidates who can pass this test.

Bottom line, if we want to significantly diminish poverty in Philippine society, in each election we must VOTE SMART. Vote intelligently.

If we can't or won't vote smart, then better to not vote at all. Because each wrong vote won't be just a great waste of our time, energy, and money.

Worse, each wrong vote will be a vote for more poverty, more injustice, as we help corrupt politicians stay longer in public office to amass more wealth and more power.

If we sell our votes to the highest vote-buyer, if we vote based merely on the politician s popularity and gimmicks, without considering track record and platform of governance, then best to stay home and do something productive. Or just sleep and rest. At least, we won't be helping the wrong candidates win.

INTRODUCTION

To speak for "fair trade" begs the question: What is fair trade?

There are many definitions, perhaps as many as the numerous groups worldwide advocating it. Google "fair trade" on the Internet and you instantly get a long list of definitions.

Factories lost

I have my own definition of "fair trade." It is based not on academic research and classroom discussions but on more than 50 years of directly experiencing UNFAIR TRADE - including the indescribable pain of helplessly watching all the factories I built up over several decades through backbreaking toil and self-sacrifice, employing more than 10,000 Filipino workers, shut down one by one as cheap imports — courtesy of GLOBALIZATION and LIBERALIZATION - flooded the market, destroying not just my factories but virtually the nation's entire, fledgling manufacturing sector, as well as the agricultural sector, equally bludgeoned by cheap food imports.

Then, to add insult to injury, likewise helplessly watching as my erstwhile foreign principals/partners took over ownership of the marketing and servicing companies I and my talented Filipino team had built up over several decades.

Again, they were able to legally mount the takeover because of our government's support for globalization and liberalization. This was a classic example of the folk saying *"Iba ang nagtanim, iba ang kumain"* (Others planted, others ate).

My companies shouldered all the multimillion investments, risks, and hard work during the early days when the brands of my foreign partners were still unknown in the Philippines.

Several decades later, after we were able to build up said brands to number-one rank in the Philippine market, my former partners - using globalization and liberalization as justification - conveniently took over my companies and harvested the fruits of our hard work.

Equally painful, the same kind of injustice was done on many other Filipino companies by their respective foreign "partners."

It is a definition based on more than 50 years of slugging it out as an entrepreneur in local and foreign market arenas, against gigantic competitors with financial, technological, and logistical resources far superior to mine, with awesome political connections versus my complete absence of such.

It is a definition based on my reflections on those profoundly difficult experiences, along with many readings and discussions on the subject.

It is a definition based on the many tragic cases I have witnessed of small Filipino entrepreneurs doing everything they could to make their businesses survive and prosper, only to be vanquished by global forces too large for them to handle.

To my mind, the best way to start a clear definition of fair trade is by defining what it is NOT, in the same way that night defines day.

What fair trade is not, its exact opposite, is the unholy duo of "free" trade GLOBALIZATION and LIBERALIZATION being espoused and imposed on the entire world by the World Trade Organization (WTO) through the so-called General Agreement on Tariffs and Trade (GATT).

As I have stated in several speeches, first of all, there is no such thing as "free trade."

Nothing in this world is free, least of all in trade.

The academic definition of "free trade" is that it is "a policy by which a government does not discriminate against imports or interfere with exports by applying tariffs (to imports) or subsidies (to exports) or quotas.

According to the law of comparative advantage, the policy permits trading partners mutual gains from trade of goods and services." *(source:* www.wikipedia.com*)*

In the real world, it is an open secret that all governments employ both overt (e.g., tariffs) and covert (e.g., hidden subsidies) measures to influence imports and exports to favor their respective national interests - or the interests of their respective ruling elites.

What fair trade is not

As early as 1996, during the term of former President Fidel V. Ramos (FVR), I already made the following statements in one of my speeches:

Cooperation or destruction of the weak?

The need for all of us Filipinos to become larger than ourselves has never been more urgent. At this very moment, our nation is hosting the Asia- Pacific Economic Cooperation or APEC Summit, a gathering of 18 world leaders with their respective contingents determined to push regional cooperation, bringing free trade to new heights of freedom by dismantling all protectionist bar- riers.

The basic timetable agreed upon for full lifting of protectionist trade barriers is year 2010 for developed countries like the United States and Japan, and year 2020 for developing countries like the

Philippines.

In effect, poor and backward nations are given only a 10-year "grace period" to attain the same level of market openness and competitiveness as rich and advanced nations.

Considering the tremendous lead currently enjoyed by advanced nations in terms of financial and technological resources, there is nothing gracious about this "grace period" at Ml. It appears to be but a token of gesture of consideration.

The situation is made worse by the current administration s overly ambitious plan to fully open up the Philippine economy by year 2003. To meet the 2020 deadline would already be miraculous. To think that we can make it by 2003 verges on being "mentally unable" to use a politically correct and polite term.

Supreme irony

The supreme irony here is that the staunchest advocates of free trade would not have attained their present strength if they had not been highly efficient and effective protectionists in the past, as contrasted to our limp, wimpy, unfocused, and generally poor protectionist policies and programs that didn't work.

Winner-take-all

Really, it's like heavyweight champion Evander Holyfield challenging a malnourished, light-as-a-feather, and poorly trained boxer from Tawi-Tawi to a championship match in Las Vegas. If Holyfield would pick on someone of equal weight, nutrition, and training, it would be a great fight. Otherwise, it will only be pathetic and tragic.

Similarly, in a level playing field, free trade would be beautiful and would unleash our best potentials. But in a highly lopsided situation, the implications are obviously ominous, - portentous of grave danger.

As a businessman-friend of mine noted: "This is actually a winner-take-all situation. Of course, big business will win, small businesses will be wiped out."

Cardinal Sin

*It is not much different from the Laurel-Langley Agreement in the early days of our nation's independence when Filipinos and Americans were theoretically given equal rights to do business and own property in each other's country. **The catch was no Filipino could afford to do business in the US.** As a result, only American businessmen benefited from the Agreement since they had all the resources needed to exploit the Philippines.*

*Cardinal Sin (Archbishop of Manila) has said that **the principal goal of APEC is profit for the strong nations.***

For such a statement, he has been criticized by the proponents of APEC as not having studied the matter thoroughly and of being narrow-minded.

If it be so, I must ask: Have the most avid supporters of APEC with its fast-track liberalization policies and programs also studied the matter thoroughly? Have they considered all the key details beyond the easy rhetoric, considering that there's much truth in the saying that the devil lies in the details?

Intellectual property

For example, the matter of "protection of intellectual property rights" under which multinational companies with their sophisticated legal and financial resources, can easily patent even indigenous technologies, so that even herbal medicines like "pito-pito" and "lagundi," long used by generations of poor Filipinos as cheaper alternative medicine will suddenly become branded and unaffordable.

While it is correct to protect intellectual property just like physical property, how do we prevent abuse of its provisions by powerful interests who will take advantage of the ignorance of backward peoples?

Furthermore, have the APEC proponents thoroughly studied the implications on the. poor and weak sectors? Have they truly provided adequate safety nets? Where are they? What are they? How will the transition be effected to ensure that liberalization will redound to the Filipino good?

We should listen to all voices in our society, especially the voice of the weak.

Is it good for the Filipino?

What I understand is if the APEC regional cooperation will indeed create the right conditions for shared growth and shared prosperity, then we should work for it, with it, in it, with all our heart and soul. We must be clear, though, on how shared growth and shared prosperity will be translated into our daily lives.

But if we ask ourselves the bottom line question — "Is it good for the Filipino?" - and find that the answer is "Not sure" or "Not clear," not necessarily "No," then we must proceed with caution and study all the detailed implications.

RP-WTO agreement (1994)

Only two years ago (1994), our President, Fidel V. Ramos, signed our adherence to WTO, subjecting us to their rules and regulations. Many critics had varying opinions on this act. Some say that he has hastily signed to something not well studied and well informed to the public, thus bringing us to more difficulties; some say that he did this out of his great belief that it's about time we learn to work globally, competitively, and Filipinos can do it, is his slogan. Some say that he did it out of his "kayabangan" (boastfulness). We will always have varying critics.

But I say, let us not be arrested in our concern for our people's welfare. We must be vigilant. We must be aware of the consequences of what is in store for us and must voice out continuing wrongdoings, good deeds, and bad governance. We must all understand the implications of globalization, liberalization, and deregulation and not forget our own national interests. Our work must be for the good of\Filipinos and our country.

I hope that the preceding points clearly explain why GLOBALIZATION and LIBERALIZATION are the exact opposite of FAIRTRADE.

If globalization and liberalization, as currently practiced, exemplify what fair trade is NOT, what then is fair trade?

I believe that "fair trade" should be defined as a system of exchange (buying and selling) of goods and services between nations/corporations with the following basic characteristics:

- Aimed at providing equitably shared benefits to all parties concerned (as opposed to a system wherein virtually all of the benefits/profits go to the wealthier and more powerful nations/corporations);

- Based on mutual respect and consideration for each other's strengths and limitations (as opposed to a systern wherein rich nations use every opportunity to exploit the weaknesses of poor nations, thus driving the latter deeper into poverty and underdevelopment).

- Based on full respect for the right of all nations to fully industrialize, i.e., to fully develop their capacity to create processed/manufactured goods, instead of forever being a source/exporter of raw materials for industrialized countries, as well as a buyer/importer/dumping ground of finished goods from said countries.

- Founded on the principle that fair competition should be based not just on compliance with the same trading rules, but also on relatively equal capabilities between the competitors - in the same manner that you don't pit a heavyweight boxer against a featherweight. Based not just on financial profitability considerations, but also on environmental, ethical, and legal considerations - not just for the present generation but also for suc-ceeding generations.

CONTENTS

I

The User-Supplier Link in Enterprise Development: A Philippine Experience

Presentation at a Session of the United Nations Conference on Trade and Development (UNCTAD) in Geneva, Switzerland, January 20, 1997

Thank you for inviting me to this important gathering.

In the MIDRAND DECLARATION after the ninth session of the United Nations Conference on Trade and Development (UNCTAD IX) held in Midrand, South Africa, from April 27 to May 11, 1996, the basic mandate of UNCTAD was reiterated: UNCTAD *"must build upon its comparative advantage and offer support appropriate to the needs of developing countries to ensure that they participate in the world economy on a more equitable basis."*

For entrepreneurs like me from the Philippines, a poor developing country that needs every support it can get to participate in the world economy on a more equitable basis, the UNCTAD mandate is like sweet music, so welcome to our ears.

It is also particularly relevant to the topic you assigned to me: "The Role of the User-Supplier Link in Enterprise Development: A Philippine Experience."

Since UNCTAD is supposed to "offer support appropriate to the needs of developing countries," on behalf of my fellow entrepreneurs, my fellow users and suppliers in developing countries, let me take advantage of UNCTAD's generous offer by focusing my talk on our most urgent need: Our need to survive.   .   .

Two-edged sword

Perhaps the two most important words in the English language now are "globalization" and "liberalization." Both are two-edged swords. One edge good, the other bad.

In discussing the role of the user-supplier link in enterprise development, especially in the context of developing nations, clearly the first question to address is how the users and suppliers in these countries can survive globalization and liberalization.

After all, if they do not survive, there would be nothing to discuss about their role in enterprise development.

Why is survival an issue relative to globalization and liberalization? I cannot improve on the answer given by UNCTAD itself in its MIDRAND DECLARATION, so again let me quote:

"Our economies continue to be unified by flows of trade, finance,

information, and technological change. This increased inter-dependence is a powerful impetus to liberalization of these flows. Competitive pressure on all economies has increased, and the market forces play a pivotal role. The rules-based system of the World Trade Organization (WTO) will facilitate positive integration of countries into the global trading system if the commitment to this objective is strengthened.

"However, we must recognize that countries enter this system from very different starting points. Accordingly, the impact of globalization and liberalization is uneven. There are notable developing country successes where domestic reforms have provided increased dynamism to international trade and investment. Yet there remains problems of access to markets, capital and technology, and many grapple with the institutional transformation necessary for meaningful integration into the world economy.

"The least developed countries (LDCs) particularly those in Africa, and other developing countries remain constrained by weak supply capabilities and are unable to benefit from trade. Marginalization, both among and within countries, has been ex-acerbated. Too many people continue to live in dire poverty. As we near the new millennium, this is an intolerable situation.

"It is in the interest of all countries that a mutually beneficial multilateral trading system continues to develop. This requires the recognition of differential impacts on countries and the solidarity necessary to ensure that all will benefit - a true partnership for development."

With the issue of survival in the context of globalization and liberalization clearly defined, let me now share with you some of my personal experiences as an entrepreneur to concretize the role of the user-sup- plier link in enterprise development.

My flagship company is more than thirty years old and together with affiliates, employ a current manpower complement of over 4,000.

We are primarily involved in the manufacture and distribution of consumer electronic products, serving both our domestic and export markets, under two of the most reputable brands in the world, Sony and Aiwa.

We are also in aqua-culture, car manufacturing and distribution.

What originally started as a trading activity evolved into manufacturing operations. Quite naturally, with the nature of our businesses, we deal with various suppliers, both local and foreign.

But before I go any further, allow me to walk you through the early years of our enterprise.

Trader to manufacturer

As I pointed out earlier, we started as traders before we were manufacturers. Our early days as traders were relatively simpler in terms of the management and deployment of resources.

By nature, a trader provides a link, where there is none, between the producer and the consumer. We were no different.

For us then, it was simply a matter of feeling what the market needed or wanted and finding the supplier who could satisfy those needs and wants.

Even with this early simplistic model, it was clear that the supplier and the entrepreneur had their own respective concerns and responsibilities: the supplier for the quality of its products, and the entrepreneur for the development and expansion of markets for the products.

We were thus then engaged, quite successfully, in the introduction of pioneering products in the Philippine market, albeit, on a slow, gradual basis.

Products like a kerosene-fueled lamp that burned brightly for hours, specialty glass products for various industries, and eventually the first Sony transistor radios were introduced to the Philippine market because we first saw the need and the means to satisfy such needs.

Expand markets and suppliers

There is no telling how big a role the products played in our seemingly successful efforts at that time. On our part, we realized that the expansion of markets was the primary consideration. Sourcing the products through a reliable network of suppliers was another.

As in any developing, small market, the thought of going into local production was hardly given any thought simply because the, scale and size of the market would not have justified investments in capital assets.

We were not only the users of the product, but also the distributors. As such^ concerns about quality quite easily passed on to the supplier. Our concerns then were different. We were concerned with prices and terms of payment, and delivery schedules.

But that early, too, we were already especially aware of our responsibility to protect and uphold the integrity of the brands and product names of the items we sold. While it was true that we did not manufacture the products, we were responsible for introducing these to the customers and therefore had the implied obligation to guarantee the products' performance.

In short, we believed in what we sold and we are certain that our suppliers appreciated this gesture.

Indeed, the foundations of a lasting relationship between the user and supplier is mutual respect for each other's products, processes, and practices.

In due time our markets expanded and we were first granted a manufacturing license in the early seventies. To us, this meant a whole new and more complicated way of doing things. We were now in a position to add considerable value to a product and positively contribute to our economic development, provide jobs to and enhance the quality of life of a vastly significant number of individuals.

In this new role as a manufacturer, our concerns and relationship with suppliers quite naturally assumed new dimensions.

We were no longer just middlemen, but users of technology and processes, as well as products. Of course, the usual, traditional concerns were still there like quality, prices, and delivery. There were however new and formidable areas we had to consider.

Make or buy?

As a manufacturer-user, we were concerned about attaining certain efficiencies to bring down our costs. Lacking the economies of scale, as is normally the case in a developing market such as ours, we were almost always confronted with a "make-or-buy" decision every time we review each component that went into our products.

In analyses of this sort, the role of the supplier weighs heavily on the future directions of the enterprise.

The supplier almost always has the technology and how far a supplier is willing to share and transfer technology has long-term implications on the development of the enterprise and how reasonably priced are their parts.

After all, the supplier can opt to merely continue supplying finished products, rather than the means to produce such products.

Even under normal circumstances, the manufacturer-user has little choice but to expand its market base, both local and foreign (but foreigners absolutely suppliers' prerogative) and hopefully in the process also gain access to the most efficient technology either through research or technology transfer.

Government attempts

This fact is not lost on governments, including ours and there had been efforts on the part of our policy makers to encourage efforts towards this end through some sort of complementation programs, especially among related industries in various countries.

Our country's car program, for example, requires each participant to manufacture certain components not just for the domestic market but for the foreign market as well. That this scheme is seemingly working is because it is an enforced condition, and so far has seen nil success in ASEAN.

Another program now in the early stages of implementation is the ASEAN Industrial Cooperation Scheme or AICO which aims to promote joint manufacturing industrial activities between ASEAN-based companies. Under this scheme, a cooperative arrangement is forged between at least two participating companies from two different ASEAN countries involving not only the physical movement of products between the two companies and countries but also resource sharing, pooling, and/or industrial complementation. This, too, has shown nil successes.

Reasons for failure

There are however reasons why such programs could fail and did fail. Affiliated companies, belonging to a vast global network, may not have problems dispersing manufacturing operations of specific components. The ready global market available to these factories does not exist for the independent manufacturer-user, who still has to develop its own markets.

As if this is not formidable enough, there is still the concern for the level of technological sophistication to be attained to be globally competitive.

In the absence of a credible research and development program, the manufacturer-user can only hope that the supplier will be willing to share technology.

Otherwise, the manufacturer-user will never be able to break from the present "screw-type" operations, which characterize most so-called manufacturing operations in developing operations in developing countries. The real value added consists of labor which, unfortunately, almost always have to be the cheapest to make economic sense and justify continued operations.

It is not difficult then to see how a seemingly entrenched and successful manufacturing operation can suddenly be rendered irrelevant because the supplier controlled a significant portion of production inputs.

Lest I be misunderstood, we have had mutually beneficial relationships with our suppliers all these years. We are confident in the thought that we have secured markets for their products, promoted their brands, and adhered to their standards of quality and efficiency. Our success has also been theirs as, ultimately, it is the supplier who make the real profits.

Certainly, our link to our suppliers contributed to the growth and success of our enterprise and we wish this mutually beneficial relationship to continue indefinitely into the future.

Disturbing questions

At this point, I would like to point to some fairly recent developments which may be of interest to you and may have some future bearing on user-supplier relationships.

In November 1996, the Philippines 4th APEC leaders' meeting, APEC, or Asia Pacific Economic Cooperation, is one among the several trade blocs organized in recent years to foster, among others, trade facilitation and trade liberalization. The globalization of trade envisions a market without borders where the vestiges of protectionism are supposed to be things of the past, with greater opportunities for the increased sale of goods and services in a vastly expanded market place.

While there is cause for guarded optimism, there are questions begging answers with respect to existing manufacturer-users who may have succeeded in developing a market for a product yet failed to fully integrate production processes, having merely been an assembler of sorts all these years.

No value for market development?

That a product succeeded in the market place is undoubtedly because of the product itself as well as the efforts to promote it, including but not limited to, the support services behind the successful marketing effort.

Markets are not built overnight, especially in the face of intense competition. Very often, it takes years of trying to understand market sentiments and perceptions, developing distribution networks, promotions, and consumer research. In all these activities, the supplier of products or technology may or may not have been actively involved.

It is the manufacturer-user who often endures the long, arduous efforts required in market development. With tariff barriers falling and the movement of goods and services across borders virtually assured, the one who possess the technology and the process clearly has the edge. That there is a ready market, developed by someone else, through years of hard work, is clearly enough motivation to disregard past relationships which may have worked perfectly in the past.

It is relatively easy to value a product: the materials and other inputs, the research and development costs, the related licenses, patents, and trademarks - all these are within the realm of exactitude and can be assigned values to.

The other intangible that makes for a successful enterprise, namely the efforts to develop markets, may not be as easily valued, and consequently, stand the risk of being altogether forgotten in the rush towards globalization.

How does one value, for example, hardship and sacrifice spent on promoting a product, dealing with fickle markets, contending with government bureaucracy, and other myriad problems inherent in developing economies?

Globalization is not an excuse to sweep aside a past which help built the present. Enterprises which all these years built businesses in tandem and cooperation with suppliers should not be swept aside simply because these suppliers now have the option of going straight to the market.

Threat

There is an obvious threat to the dignity of a nation and its enterprise if, under the guise of globalization, erstwhile suppliers of production inputs now decide to disregard further investments in the host country, simply because the floodgates are open. This is not what globalization is all about and it certainly is not the kind of supplier-user link that encourages enterprise development.

There could well be a rush of joint venture agreements encouraged by the movement towards trade liberalization. This is well and good for as long as the joint venture involves the sharing and pooling of resources, from technology to hard assets. A joint venture designed merely to exploit markets with hardly any investment is likewise not the kind that decency and fairness contemplate.

This conference and gatherings like this provide-us opportunities to discuss issues and concerns such as the ones I have presented.

As I have earlier intimated, the MIDRAND DECLARATION is most reassuring to developing economies, especially the marginalized ones.

There are concerns enough for developing enterprises which, because of the inequities in trade, will fail even before they can succeed.

As if this is not tragedy enough, we ought to shudder further at the thought that not only emerging enterprises and economies are in danger, but enterprises which have grown and developed, and currently employ thousands can be pushed to extinction once their markets are raided in the name of globalization.

Globalization and liberalization

Hand in hand with globalization is liberalization. While globalization is supposed to bring about some utopian dream of bringing about global economic stability and equitable dispersal of wealth to benefit also the poor countries, this was immediately negated by the rapid liberalization of goods and services where tariffs, subsidies were drastically and rapidly reduced without any safety nets put in by those "genius" bureaucrats who relied on theories, books, rhetoric to make this new phenomenon called globalization the new model. Our economic advisers believed in the WTO and IMF as the authority on this new concept.

It is our wish that this concern be also considered in UNCTAD's agenda and declarations.

We may not have the answers today but we are nevertheless hopeful that future policies of governments and leaders who believe in universal principles of fairness and equity will be enlightened by the policies and recommendations of this August assembly.

Once again, let me express my deepest appreciation for the time to speak to you today.

Thank you and good afternoon.

II
A Friendship of More Than a Thousand Years: Welcome Remarks for Mr. Xi Jin Ping

Formal dinner at Manila Hilton Hotel, 1991
NOTE:

Life is strange. Who would have known that the middle-level Chinese official who visited our Solid factories here in the Philippines in 1991 would, 21 years later, become the President of China?

Mr. Xi Jin Ping's visit to the Philippines came about after he toured the factories (for TV, video, audio products) established by my husband, Joseph, in China, particularly in Shenzhen and Xiamen.

Actually, Joseph was the first Filipino-Chinese entrepreneur to set up factories in China during the seventies to eighties, when China was just starting to fast-track its economic development. Many years later, other Filipino-Chinese businessmen also invested in China, following the path which Joseph pioneered.

At that time, Mr. Xi Jin Ping was the First Secretary of Fuzhou City. During the tour he made at our China factories, he was pleased at the sight of thousands of Chinese workers employed there. When Joseph told him that we have similar factories in the Philippines and invited him to come for a visit, he readily accepted.

Towards the end of his Philippine visit, we hosted a dinner in his honor at the Manila Hilton Hotel. Around two hundred guests joined us. Below are my brief Welcome Remarks:

Good evening and thank you, dear friends, for taking time to join us tonight in this special dinner for our esteemed guest, Mr. Xi Jin Ping, the First Secretary of Fuzhou City, capital of Fujian Province in Southern China.

In welcoming him to our country, I am somehow reminded of a few interesting, historical facts about the relationship between the Philippines and her foreign visitors.

When the Spaniards came to our shores in 1521, we fought. When the British came in 1762, we fought. When the, Americans came in 1896, we fought. When the Japanese came in 1941, we also fought.

Curiously, the only foreign visitors we never fought were those who came even hundreds of years earlier than the Spaniards: Our Chinese friends and trading partners, who visited us as early as 971 A.D., more than 500 years before the Spanish conquistadores entered our shores.

Instead of fighting them, we embraced them and they embraced us back, not only in friendship but also in love. Proof of the latter are the millions of Filipino-Chinese who trace their roots to the loving marriages and relationships which took place between the Chinese visitors and their native hosts. Filipino-Chinese who have given the very best of their talents, even their very lives, in service to the Filipino nation, as public servants, entrepreneurs, professionals - even as revolutionaries and guerrillas in the war against Spanish, British, American, and Japanese colonizers.

Perhaps the reason why, for more than a thousand years now, we have maintained a peaceful, productive, and friendly relationship with our Chinese guests is the fact that they never tried to exploit or colonize us, unlike the others who came calling.

Instead, they have always tried to become an integral part of the local economy, providing much-needed products, services, and technology, at the most affordable prices for the ordinary Filipino.

It is therefore not surprising that Filipinos have welcomed them with great warmth and sincerity for more than a thousand years.

It is in this context of a great friendship of more than a thousand years that we warmly welcome our dear friend and guest, First Secretary Xi Jin Ping.

NOTE:

After my Welcome Remarks, Mr. Xi Jin Ping gave a brief response in Chinese, which was translated into English for the benefit of the non-Chinese listeners.-

I look back with deep appreciation at the simple words of wisdom he shared with us.

First, he expressed his gratitude to me and my husband, as well as to Solid Corporation, for inviting him to visit the Philippines.

Then he expressed his admiration and appreciation at the efficiency and productivity of the Filipino workers in Solid's factories.

He emphasized the deep ties of friendship and partnership, going back to more than a thousand years, between the Philippines and China.

He noted that trade between both countries has prospered through the years because it has always been marked by fairness, mutual trust, and mutual benefit.

China is committed to building a new world order founded on peace, harmony, justice, and shared prosperity among all nations, he said.

In conclusion, he called on everyone to support and help in establishing such a world order.

Now that he is the incoming President of China, a nation with the world's largest population (1.35 billion, or 19.1% of the seven billion total world population as of 2011), a leader with the authority and resources to put into concrete action the laudable ideals he shared with us 21 years ago, I sincerely wish him success in all his endeavors.

The world we live in now is mired in violence, wars within and between nations, and the threat of bigger wars.

It seems that after two world wars which killed and crippled millions of human beings and destroyed billions of dollars worth of precious assets, human beings are still as stupid, shortsighted, narrow-minded, and. greedy as ever.

It seems that two world wars are not enough lesson for us.

When will we ever learn the folly of war and violence?

When will we ever learn that human life is absolutely sacred and priceless, that nothing in this world, no material gain, cdn ever justify killing people?

When will we ever learn that violence can only lead to more violence?

I have personally experienced the Second World War and, believe me, war is absolute hell.

Instead of finding ways to resolve conflicts and competing interests through peaceful dialogue, instead of using the power of new information technology to become closer and kinder to each, nations and peoples now find themselves in endless arms race, wasting more and more of their precious funds on the most criminal weapons of war which enrich only the merchants of death.

Now, more than ever, for the sake of present and future generations, we desperately need wise and great leaders dedicated to peace and goodwill.

III
The Principles that Make Dreams Reality

Rotary Club of Manila Century Park Sheraton Hotel, Manila February 22, 1996

As we look around us today, it seems that philosophers and politicians are already in great supply, but achievers and perfectionists, dedicated to doing their best, are still rare sights, if not endangered species.

I say this because it seems to be the fashion to accept the status quo of corruption, inefficiency and ineffectiveness in our society, particularly in our government.

Share a passion to overcome difficulties

Let me share with you a small but tremendously important bit of information: We can become the society we dream of!

We can overcome our current problems, no matter how seemingly insurmountable!

I know because I have seen it done. I am a witness to man's victory over the worst of adversaries, whether it be the forces of nature or the elements spawned by the darker side of human nature. Yes, my friends, we can become the society we dream of.

Needed: Honest soul

The root of our country's problems is that we have lost our common foundations of basic human and social values.

What is required is neither technology nor psychoanalysis but an honest soul searching to rediscover what is good, decent and fair in each of us and as a people.

It is only when this happens that we will begin to see significant systems reform in the various sectors of society.

Shared values will translate into transparent and fair systems. Systems reforms. Fair systems. Sounds too good to be true? Not if we all begin by embracing a simple truth - - that all of us share in the responsibility to deal with the present problems and share in the price of reform.

We must stand together and carry out our various endeavors guided by the same principles and values. A problematic sector of our society will reform if the rest of us deal with it with firm consistency and unity. Like the phalanx of the Roman legions, none should break ranks. A strong solid front will push back the strongest foes who will not find any crack to slip through.

Let me now share with you some of the key principles that have led me to find success both in business and in helping to build the foundation of our Filipino values.

Demand integrity!

Somerset Maugham once said:

"It's a funny thing about life; if you refuse to accept anything but the best, you often get it."

I believe the same is true for integrity and honesty. We must demand integrity in all our dealings!

There must be no room for compromise of the solid front will collapse in the face of an enemy assault. There is corruption and abuse because we do not demand integrity of ourselves and of others.

In my own organization, we are very supportive of our management team, allowing great latitude for experimentation and growth. But I have taken to task senior managers for cases of even minor misuse of funds.

No one should be exempted from the demand of integrity. Employees should be made aware of the moral standards they are expected to maintain in all their dealings, and government dealings are no exception.

Corrupt and abusive government bureaucrats and officials think they can get away with things because they divide and conquer those they victimize, especially businesses that are pressured by deadlines and commitments.

But if enough of the business community would stand together to demand integrity in government service, then there would no longer be a place for terrible government service.

If not terrible, then at its very best, a much delayed and inefficient service which causes injury to the lives of our people.

Every unjust delay, every unreasonable inaction is an injury to the Filipino. Government mouths flowery motherhood statements of partnership between government and business under the guise of some loose consultative process.

One visible standard practice of government is to fix things for us as they deem fit and it becomes our duty to comply. There is an apparent lack of genuine concern to create the right atmosphere for the private sector to achieve their goals and objectives with professional efficiency. Thus, the partnership is not real.

Many times there is no integrity in government pronouncements and implementation. We should not submit meekly to government "fixes" affecting our lives. Demand integrity!

Invest in people

Now, if we agree that rediscovering and strengthening our same sense of principles and values are the keys to the building of our' society, then we must agree with the next principle:

We invest in people, not things.

After all, Charles Rouce once wrote, "Not in time, place, or circumstance, but in man lies success."

This seems straightforward enough but many find it is not as easy to do.

You see, products don't sell products. People do. Technology doesn't make itself. People do. Before products could satisfy a customer's needs, there must first be a salesperson who sold him the right product at the right price with the right attitude.

It is our people who must bear the brunt of the everyday battle of building business and family and we must strive to help them do both.

Build good business and build fine Filipino families. We must train our people not just in skills because they would be heartless machines. We must participate in their social and personal formation so that they too will be equipped to meet the demands of integrity and pay its stringent price.

Development of [1] human resources

Training is not a matter of finding an HRD manager. Involvement must come from the very top and span to the very bottom of the organization.

Whenever there is an orientation and values training program conducted in one of my companies located at the Clark Special

Economic Zone, I make it a point to attend and speak to the new employees about the values that built the company and continue to guide it.

The last day of the training always includes the family of the new employees and I try to talk to their families as well to share with them the vision of what we are to achieve in the company. The result is a strong and cohesive workforce that has achieved miracle after miracle including breaking into the prestigious Japanese electronics market. Not that there will be no disappointments with people along the way, but I am a firm believer of the innate goodness of man and I refuse to be discouraged by a few exceptions.

CDC experience

Recently, I have found myself in a new struggle where I have to make my voice heard. But thankfully I am no longer alone.

Some of you may be aware that I am a part of a group of more than thirty active manufacturers/investors/locators in the Clark Special Economic Zone that is calling for the immediate suspension of the long list of manual of fees that are made to bear upon us by the Clark Development Corporation without any consultative process.

Under other circumstances, investors might have just accepted the new imposition of CDC and tried to make the most of the situation.

In less than two weeks, my company alone has paid quite a substantial amount just for fees for bureaucratic paper requirements.*

However, we found our voice! And it is an even stronger one because we all have the same voice and message.

We have found the strength to demand integrity in the solid phalanx of unity we formed. (The battle is still going on. We will have a meeting tomorrow.) But I feel victory has already been won because we have taken a stand based on the principles of goodness and fairness and nothing can stop us now.

Today, we also hear various voices coming from some sectors who do so for personal gain, for political gimmickry, for grandstanding activities, for all sorts of wheeling and dealing at the expense of innocent persons and to the injury of our people.

These are not the voices to be heard or to be listened to. It must be the voice of the oppressed, whether it be from the rich or the poor, fighting for decency, fairness and justice.

My friends, remember, it doesn't matter how many you are because it only takes one man of courage to form a majority! The greatest example is our Lord Jesus Christ. My last principle is a poetic one.

Persist in your vision

The flow of the gentlest stream will eventually wear down the hardest rock, not because of strength, but because of persistence.

Clinging tightly to your vision and letting nothing dissuade you from your mission is the principle I want to talk about now. We have a lesson to learn from the gentle stream — the lesson of Persisting In Your Vision.

Goodness can be found in the most discouraging situation so long as there is a vision to see beyond the shade.

Let us live by these principles: *Demand integrity.*

Invest in people.

Find your voice.

Persist in your vision.

> **The CDC fees were later suspended to the satisfaction of all the Clark locators/investors.*

IV

Globalization Must Mean Humanization

Keynote Speech at the Philippine launching of the United Nations Development Programme's (UNDP) "1999 Human Development Report"; EDSA Plaza Hotel, Mandaluyong City, July 1999

"What have we done?"

At 8:15 A.M. on August 6, 1945, a plane named Enola Gay dropped an atomic bomb on Hiroshima. As he witnessed Hiroshima's obliteration, Captain Robert Lewis, co-pilot of the Enola Gay, asked himself: "My God, what have we done?" Six billion human beings now live on earth. Meeting their basic needs is hard enough. Today we have embarked on a globalization program which is increasingly concentrating economic wealth, political power, knowledge, and technology in the elite 1/5, or 1.2 billion, of the world's population, while making 4/5, or 4.8 billion people, live in limbo and uncertainty. As I ponder on the long-term implications of this trend, I find myself asking the same question as Captain Lewis: My God, what have we done?

Definition of Development

The United Nations Development Programme (UNDP) **defines human development as the process of enlarging people's choices — not just on what detergents or soft drinks they can buy — but on what they can do with their lives.**

Measured by this standard, globalization as we now know it is doing the opposite: By making more people poorer, it is reducing, not enlarging, people's choices on what they can do with their lives. Indeed, beggars can't be choosers.

Development: Central goal

The bottom line of the 1999 Human Development Report of UNDP is that unless human development, instead of profit, is made the central goal of globalization, then it will only be a matter of time—possibly just a few more years — before the gap between the haves and have-nots, the know and know-nots, reaches cataclysmic proportions.

The architects of globalization seem to have been blinded by the immense profits being generated by their scheme. They seem to have forgotten a very important lesson from history: There is a limit to the suffering that even the most timid people will bear.

But perhaps a more positive and compelling argument for those who see only the business side of globalization is that in the long term, it makes perfect business sense to make human development the central goal of globalization. It is best to do business in a peaceful and stable market environment, wherein majority are gainfully employed and have adequate purchasing power.

There are many paths to globalization and liberalization. The subject is laden with technicalities, legalities, and contradictions. However, in my view, there are several basic guideposts to the right path.

Avoid simplistic debates

First, we should stop reducing the discussion to a simplistic black-and-white debate, as though one is either for globalization or protectionism. Our discussions will become more productive if we focus on finding the right mix of grays between different perspectives.

Avoid forcing uniform timetables

Second, we should remember that the world's 174 nations cannot march into globalization and liberalization at a uniform or structured pace, precisely because they are not uniform or structurally acceptable, much less reachable.

The time limit set by the World Trade Organization (WTO) is absolutely unrealistic because these nations have vastly different levels of development, Each has unique characteristics.

Globalization's aim: Development for all?

Forcing them to meet uniform set timetables for participation in global competition can only lead to the destruction of economies which are not yet in a position to compete globally.

I am of course presuming that it is not the intent of globalization to destroy such nations. The question of whether competitiveness can foster human development is particularly relevant at this point.

Cart-before-horse globalization: The cruelest scam of all.

Even the most intellectually-challenged supporter of globalization can perhaps understand that if you place the cart in front of the horse, the Cart will not move. You have to reverse the sequence, place the cart behind the horse, so the horse can pull the cart.

In the same manner, the cart of globalization (unrestricted flow of goods between countries) can only move properly if it is placed behind a horse composed of nations with relatively equal economic capabilities.

For as long as there is a very large imbalance or inequality in the economic production capabilities of the world's nations, insisting on globalization is like putting the cart in front of the horse.

More accurately, it's like putting the cart before nothing, since the absence of nations with relatively equal competitive capabilities means there's even no horse to speak of.

Insisting on globalization in such a situation will not lead to free trade and fair competition.

It can only lead to the annihilation of the local industries of poor nations who simply do not have the resources to compete against the gigantic multinational corporations (MNCs) of First World nations.

It can only lead to the loss of millions of local jobs (and greater poverty for the families of displaced workers) as the local industries close shop.

It can only lead to more bankruptcies for local farmers and agricultural producers as they find themselves unable to compete with cheap vegetable and meat products from rich nations, who enjoy the advantage of large government subsidies (to lower cost) and highly mechanized production.

It can only lead to even greater monopoly of wealth and power by MNCs and their home-govemments, at the expense of poor nations.

It can only mean the rich getting richer and the poor getting poorer.

"Free Trade" = Death of local businesses.

When a rich nation pressures a poor nation to allow the unlimited tax-free entry of the rich nation's products, using "free trade" as justification, then it means the death of small local industries that simply don't have the financial, technological, and managerial resources to compete. The economies of scale which enable MNCs to produce large quantities of high-quality goods at low cost and sell at low prices are simply beyond the reach of local industries just starting out.

When it becomes cheaper to import goods than to produce them locally, then the only option left for local manufacturers is to close shop and lay off workers. Unfortunately, only local manufacturers offer local jobs (imported goods are produced by workers in other nations).

Protection for rich nations only?

It should be noted that all the advanced economies passed through a protectionist stage before they reached their present status. Their economies did not become strong overnight.

For several decades, they had to protect their local industries by restricting or preventing the entry of foreign products into the local market, and by strictly limiting foreign ownership or participation in local business. And now that they are already strong, they are suddenly changing the rules of the game. Protectionism is suddenly wrong. They are pressuring young and weak economies to immediately compete in the global arena, without benefit of enough time to build their infrastructures to let their local industries mature.

Indeed, all the nice-sounding statements to justify the imposition of cart-before-horse globalization on poor nations are simply deliberate lies to conceal the fact that globalization is another term for greater monopoly of wealth and power by rich nations, at the expense of poor nations.

Competitiveness should not be an illusion

I do believe that healthy and fair competition can foster human development, in that it encourages people to continually surpass themselves.

But the competitiveness being fostered by the present program of globalization and liberalization appears to be something else. It applies only to advanced economies, while remaining an illusion for backward economies.

Allow me to illustrate this point with a doll *(I showed the audience a traditional "Russian Doll," i.e., a doll with many smaller look-alike dolls hidden inside it)*.

This doll *(biggest doll)* represents the top 20% of the world's population living in advanced economies such as the United States, Canada, Australia, Japan, Germany, France, Netherlands, Belgium, the Scandinavian countries, United Kingdom, and the like. They hold 97% of all patents worldwide, 86% of the world's Gross Domestic

Product, 82% of world export markets, 91% of all internet users, 74% of telephone lines, and 71% of global trade in goods and services.

The other countries have to struggle desperately against each other for the remaining slices of the global pie.

The second 20% of the world's 174 nations *(I uncovered the smaller second doll)* is composed of countries — whom we can perhaps describe in more familiar terms as upper middle class — like the Czech Republic, Bahrain, Singapore, Hungary, Thailand, Malaysia, etc.

The third 20% *(I uncovered the third smallest doll)* is composed of middle class countries like the Philippines, China, Russian Federation, Brazil, Jordan, etc.

The fourth 20% (fourth smallest doll) are lower middle-class countries like El Salvador, Vietnam, Egypt, and Iraq.

The bottom 20% *(I uncovered the last and smallest doll)* are the lower class countries like Sudan, Nigeria, Haiti, Ethiopia, and Sierra Leone.

Through these dolls we can see how lopsided the competition is.

Demotion more likely

The smaller dolls represent nations which do not have the minimum macro and micro economic conditions required to compete globally.

How can a pre-industrial country compete against post-industrial countries? The proponents of globalization say that by competing, these small dolls will become big dolls. But I think it is easier for these medium-sized dolls to end up like the smallest doll. *(I held up the biggest and the smallest dolls).*

Action without Vision

A wise leader once said: "Vision without action is a daydream. Action without vision is a nightmare."

In my view, the leaders of developing countries who signed up their nations as eager participants of the globalization and liberalization program administered by the World Trade Organization did so in a classic example of action with very short vision. The best example is the Philippines.

Nor did they anticipate that even mature economies like Japan, Korea, and Hong Kong are not capable of absorbing sudden massive capital inflows and outflows. What more with immature economies? Such volatility led to the recent traumatic Asian meltdown which started in Thailand.

Development as central goal

Indeed, we cannot stop information technology as it globalizes not only business but also culture, politics, and crime.

What we can do, though, is unite in making the world's decision makers realize that it makes perfect business and political sense to make human development, not profit, the central goal of globalization.

In closing, let me say that for globalization to succeed, wealth, resources, technology MUST be made affordable, accessible, and available to the poor nations and its poof people. It must not be used to exploit them further by all sorts of hidden agenda under the guise of "modem protectionism" where the rich and powerful are favored and exempted from their own crafted WTO rules where "subsidies" exist when it is for their own national interests.

Rich can't understand poor

This globalization "solution" foisted on us by the World Trade Organization (WTO), an elite organization of four to five great countries, certainly cannot understand the hearts of the weak and the poor. They understand power, wealth, conquests, and domination.

It is no wonder that to date, all annual meetings of the WTO have been met with protests, anger, even violence.

Even their own citizens have gone to the streets protesting against possible loss of jobs as cheap imports force local industries to close.

If so, how much more for their much poorer brothers and sisters living in Third World status? Where do they go? They have been impoverished to the point that many have turned to criminal acts just to survive.

A simple solution

There is a solution, a simple one. Those who have gained much through fair or foul means must now learn to SHARE their bounty. They must try to look at this "ONE WORLD, ONE PEOPLE," with insight and concern for "ONE," to think of "one" in terms of human beings worthy of respect and dignity, who must not be exploited, and humanity must be restored.

V

Entrepreneurship with Honor

Rotary Club of Makati Metro, District 3830; Manila Golf & Country Club, July 27, 2004

Good evening Rotary Club of Makati Metro.

As I survey this room of distinguished gentlemen, some of the best and brightest of our business community, I am encouraged and hopeful that from this gathering will spring forth leaders whom I can support in facing our country's challenges, rebuilding our economy and reinventing the way we do business.

We must reinvent not only the kinds of businesses we are to invest in, the methods we use or the technologies we apply to them. We must redefine the very spirit and principles that guide us in building these businesses. For the economic, social and political turmoil this country is facing will not be overcome by investments and economic activity alone but by business leaders guided by honor and working according to clear moral principles.

But this situation is not unique or new to us. We have had to face this before. Ever since, we have relied on certain principles to guide us. These principles have made our decision-making quick and built unity in our companies; both were critical elements for our survival.

Where did our principles come from? Where did our moral strength, to do what was right even at a terrible cost, come from? Our principles and the moral conviction to live them out came from a deeply ingrained sense of Honor.

Ladies and Gentlemen, our Honor should be made of sterner stuff than the passing adulation of sycophants and influence peddlers.

It is not the honor of public acclaim that we seek but rather a clear personal sense of principled conduct that enables us to walk away from opportunities that would have enriched us but leave us with a compromised soul.

Our Honor is not about what we receive but more about what we are willing to give up in order to keep the integrity of your principles intact.

Our honor is expressed in three guiding principles that define our very being and our priorities in life and business.

Principle 1: Pride in the Filipino at Work

Our first principle is **Pride in the Filipino at Work.** We must truly believe in the worth and potential of the Filipino and it is **our duty to pursue business policies that support this.**

In the years when it was the standard for SONY to have a Japanese in-country general manager for manufacturing, we persevered in building up our Filipino engineers to the point we were able to convince the legendary Dr. Yoshida, the inventor of the Trinitron picture tube, to allow the Filipino engineers to manage the plant operations.

The Philippines holds the distinction of being the first country to be allowed to do that. We succeeded because we made it our duty to ensure that the Filipino should be the best in his own country.

I used the word duty because it takes a deep commitment to set management policies that will train, support and challenge the Filipino to bring out the best. I am told that Filipinos excel all around the world because of the disciplined foreign work environments. Then let every businessman and professional, yes, each one of you here, make it your duty to create a disciplined and principled workplace that will instill Pride in the Filipino; where you will demand and bring out the best of the Filipino at work.

But there is another side of Pride In The Filipino.

It also means our honor is based on building our businesses through **hard work and professional capabilities.**

It is my honor and the honor of those who have worked with me, that in all my years, I have never built a business based on privilege or connection.

I have never managed a "rent-seeking" business - merely collecting someone else' hard earned profits simply because I have a political connection or I know the right person to pay.

I am proud of the Filipino and I will not degrade myself or my colleagues with lazy, non-productive and corrupt business shortcuts. Neither should any of you. All of you in this room are better than that and should strive for the greater good.

Principle 2: Enduring Honesty and Transparency

It is never enough to be just honest. We must strive to be above suspicion, for even the slightest doubt can taint the whole man. But more than this, we must demand honesty in our organization, from those we work with.

When we started the "people's car" project, we fought against the monopoly of the Japanese car manufacturers. At that time, only people of privilege could acquire cars at prices way beyond the reach of ordinary Filipinos. In every public industry hearing, powerful government officials directly opposed my efforts to break that monopoly by introducing less expensive options.

After years of public hearings and delaying tactics of the powerful lobbying efforts of those who opposed opening the market, we finally got our chance to introduce less expensive cars to the Filipino market.

But they were not finished with me yet. I was soon accused of smuggling and violating the terms of the "people's car" project. I was summoned to a witch-hunt otherwise known as a Senate committee hearing. Many counseled me to meet secretly with the Senator co-chairing the committee and "come to terms" with him. Intermediaries came to set a secret breakfast meeting. I flatly refused. My message to him was, "I will not break bread with the likes of you." I eat with friends and colleagues, not with those who perpetuate darkness, fear and corruption.

I rebuffed an offer for an easy way out of the persecution because I believed in **Enduring Honesty.** I knew I had to show others that Honesty does win when we are willing to endure challenges and trials. But to do this, I knew that I had to go to the Senate hearings to show it. I was confident because I went there, not only with an assurance that my operation was completely honest and aboveboard, but also with the confidence of **transparency.**

You see, I foresaw that there would be a possibility of further harassment so I pursued the policy of Transparency. This means that I meticulously documented the process we went through in bringing in the cars so that there would not be a slightest doubt or question about our business.

The result? The Senator chairing the committee hearing was soon so chastened by the overwhelming evidence I presented that he ended the session praising our work and claiming that the committee hearing had "successfully exonerated" me. How is that for turning the tables?

The principle here is Enduring Honesty and Transparency. We must demand this of ourselves and from those we work with. It will not be easy and sacrifices are many. But if we do not do it, do we not become part of the very problem that we bemoan?

Principle 3: Courage

C.S. Lewis said, "Courage is not simply one of the virtues but the form of **every virtue at the testing point,** which means at the point of highest reality. Courage is our third principle that keeps our honor alive.

My friends, **the highest reality is the point when opposition and challenges will exact the greatest price if we persist in pursuing our goals. Courage is keeping your mind firm** on the purposes and principles that you have adopted and remembering that they are worth much more than the price that may be paid.

I have passed that testing point again and again. I have been rejected and refused, maligned and accused, betrayed and cheated. After the December coup in 1989, I pioneered the first industrial estate in Laguna called the Laguna International Industrial Park, while all investors were in a Wait-and-see mood, but this was subjected to all sorts of harassment that delayed the implementation of my project by two years. The industrial estate developers who came after were even able to market earlier than us.

The same fate befell my People's Car Project. Instead of marketing the Kia Pride at one hundred thousand Philippine pesos (Php100,000.00), it was finally marketed at the double the original amount due to the fall of the Philippine peso and interests incurred with the delay.

In a career that spans forty years of difficulties, I have many similar stories to tell and stories that tested my will to overcome compromises that test one's soul. But in each case, I remember that I am still committed to bringing out the best in the Filipino; I am committed to conducting my businesses and myself in Honesty and Transparency. And my courage comes from remembering that one day, I will answer to a God who will value my fidelity, not my profitability and how I have helped my fellowman, not used him.

My courage also comes from knowing that there are generations that will follow us who will desperately look for heroes; everyday heroes who will decide on moral principles and values and not just based on experience. It is from us that they will draw the courage to do live their lives in honor or baseless and shallow greed. The future generations are our children and grandchildren. Their eyes are locked on what we do and their souls will be fed by the choices we make and the stands we take.

Not Perfect

I am neither perfect nor ready for sainthood. But I know I have done my best to engage in building businesses with a sense of honor that I am eager and proud to pass that on to my children and grandchildren. I know that this is the best heritage I can pass on to them - a heritage of pride in their countrymen, enduring honesty and transparency. But most of all, I want them to treasure courage - courage to stand up and pursue their businesses with honor above all else. I am sure that there is not a person in this room who does not want the same for his family as well. They need your heritage of honor more than an inheritance of money.

Let me close by sharing with you a poem that is very close to my heart and summarizes very well what I have spoken of today. These are the words of William Ernest Henley in his poem, " Invictus".

Out of the night that covers me,
Black as the Pit from pole to pole,
I thank whatever gods may be For my unconquerable soul.
In the fell clutch of circumstance I have not winced nor cried aloud.

Under the bludgeonings of chance My head is bloody, but unbowed.
Beyond this place of wrath and tears Looms but the Horror of the
shade,
And yet the menace of the years Finds, and shall find, me unafraid.
It matters not how strait the gate,
How charged with punishments the scroll, I am the master of my fate:
I am the captain of my soul.

Thank you and God bless us all!

VI
Urgent Appeal to Japan, Inc.
(the Mighty *Keidan-ren)*
NOTE:

This speech which I. delivered sometime in 1986 could well be
my most controversial speech - so controversial that all available
copies of the speech (supposed to be distributed to the audience after
the speech) were ordered confiscated, shredded, and thrown out by a
cabinet secretary of the late President Corazon C. Aquino's
administration (1986-1992).

After the talk, you could have heard a pin drop. The secretary
was so angry that he repeatedly berated me for upsetting the Japanese
guests. "How can you make such a terrible speech, Elena? We invited
them to come and invest and you make such a terrible speech!"

Taking the cue, other conference participants, Japanese and
Filipinos, ostracized me. Only a few talked to me during the post-
conference dinner. Ironically, those who did were mostly Japanese
who expressed "shock and awe" at what I said. My fellow-Filipinos
gave me the cold shoulder.

The conference was held in Manila at the Philippine
International Convention Center (PICC) in 1986, attended by about
a hundred members of the "Keidan-ren," the most powerful and
prestigious business organization in Japan, composed of chairmen
and CEOs of Japan's top multinational industrial corporations.

It was chaired by no less than the Chairman of Marubeni
Corporation and formally opened by President Aquino.

The gathering was a result of a state visit by President Aquino to
Japan, wherein she invited Japan to invest further in the Philippines.

Keidan-ren members attended to show Japan's support for the
newly-installed Aquino government, fresh from the 1986 "People

Power" bloodless uprising which toppled the infamous Marcos dictatorship which had ruled the Philippines for 20 years.

As a consistent Filipino exporter to Japan, as well as President of the Philippine Exporters Foundation (PHILEXPORT) and Philippine partner of Japan's Sony Corporation, I was the only female Filipino business leader invited to speak before the gathering of Keidan-ren executives at the Philippine International Convention Center (PICC).

My speech may have been thrown away and banned from distribution. But what I said still burns in my heart, and below is the speech that elicited, according to its listeners, both "shock and awe."
***

I must first admit to great awe and trepidation. To be invited to speak before the *Keidan-ren*, the highest advisory body of the Japanese business sector to the government of Japan, an organization composed of the most senior captains of Japanese industry, is an honor I feel truly unworthy of.   ,

That I am the only female speaker in this gathering also adds to the discomfiture. Not because I'm a woman, because I'm proud to be one, but out of awareness of Japanese customs, which still place women a notch or two below men.

Good News

For many years now, Japan has been one of the biggest development aid donors to the Philippines. The millions of dollars you provide us in the form of grants and soft loans have built not only schools, hospitals, bridges, and roads; they have also built new and better lives for millions of poor Filipinos and have likewise helped in raising the level of the economy.

Another important contribution of Japan is its active support for Philippine industrialization. Japan has played a. major role in the development of our nation's assembly and manufacturing capabilities in the auto industry, consumer electronics, to some appliances, semiconductors, and many other industries.

In the consumer electronics industry, Japanese companies have actively entered in joint ventures with existing Filipino companies, and have provided many jobs, enhanced local skills, increased revenues, and generated more tax payments.

Sony

In my personal experience, I put up a company fully owned by Filipinos and became the exclusive manufacturer and distributor of Sony products. As such, we built up the Sony brand to make it the number one household television in the Philippines.

We, too, provided many jobs, invested in our Filipino engineers and technicians to gain good technical training to manufacture, sell, and service the Sony products we made locally.

Sony opted not to invest in the Philippines but we met the challenge and invested in promoting Sony with our good relationship with Sony Japan, who helped us in our endeavors by providing us their parts and technical know-how. This good symbiotic relationship is a credit to both the pioneering spirit of the Filipinos and the technological advancement of Japan.

Japanese support for Filipino manufacturers and exporters has also been most helpful and welcome.

Personally, I am grateful for Japan being my first market for our Philippine Tiger prawn export. This has been a top dollar earner for our country and has also opened areas of countryside development.

As Sony manufacturer and distributor in the Philippines, we have gained good techniques for electronic assembly and
have provided jobs to our people. As one of our top export markets, Japan's importance to the Philippine economy cannot be overemphasized.

Tourism

Equally important, Japan has been supportive of the Philippine tourism industry. As we can see in virtually all our resorts and tourist spots, Japanese tourists abound, bringing in much-needed foreign currency and stimulating local business and employment.

Japanese tourists have become the number one visitors to our country. As a whole, there is good synergy in business relations with Japan. In fact next to the United States, Japan is our biggest business partner in the entire Asia. For these good things and many more, we say "thank you."

I say many more because more can be done, much more. There are some "flaws" in our relationship, and as I only desire that our relationship will be deepened and made more satisfying, it is but right that I mention some issues, in the hope that some improvements will follow upon full realization and correction of these flaws.

The reforms that need to be made, to improve understanding and create a fairer and more mutually beneficial relationship between the Philippines and Japan, are as follows:

Stop smuggling of RP logs into Japan

In the matter of helping the Philippines preserve her natural resources, we are saddened by statistics of log exports to Japan.

Sadder still is the disturbing allegation that official statistics are but a fraction of the actual quantity of Philippine logs smuggled into

Japan.

This allegation should be thoroughly investigated. If true, both nations should immediately act to stop the practice.

The denudation of our forests due to illegal logging has resulted in extremes of flooding and drought, bringing death and destruction, every year, to millions of Filipinos.

At the very least there should be better and more accurate communication between our countries on the actual state of the entry of Philippine logs into Japan.

I believe that business profits should always be subjugated to people's interests. Certainly, the customs bureau of Japan should easily discern the great discrepancies in their entries and should immediately inform the Philippine government about the problem.

But, of course, our own customs should be the first vigilant watchman. We cannot excuse ourselves. We allowed false entries and over-shipments.

We need the Japanese government to help us curb this greedy practice by disallowing shipments that have false entries. Likewise, if they inform our government we can remedy this by investigations at their ports with their cooperation.

Stop screw-type investments; promote deeper technology transfer

In the matter of investments made by Japan in the Philippines, especially in manufacturing concerns, business operations abroad have improved.

Your products have found a lucrative market in the Philippines but some products are not geared to long-term development.

Some are merely screw-type operations and these will not enhance our capabilities but will, actually, stunt our future growth on investments and technology transfer.

There should be more investments plowed in for further development of products, like making also the parts and accessories here instead of importing them as finished products.

There should be deeper technology transfer which will truly help build Philippine industry. The current practice of screw-type technology transfer, which reduces us to mere assemblers, should be moved to a higher level of parts manufacturing as well.

Efforts should be made to encourage your suppliers to locate their factories here. Vital parts should be made locally and not imported as finished products.

Needed: More respect for Filipino professionals

Companies are still led by Japanese executives who get much higher salaries than their Filipino counterparts.

Higher levels of management remain mostly in the hands of Japanese expats. Filipino professionals occupy middle supervisory positions despite their being graduates of top U.S. and Philippine universities and quite capable of top management positions.

They should learn to respect the work of Filipinos who can do the job just as well and Filipino managers must get salaries justly proportionate, if not equal to, what Japanese expatriates are getting.

Highly unequal salaries

On the matter of salaries and incentives, Filipino counterparts get rather low salaries because the higher management jobs are reserved for the expatriates, even though Filipino professionals can do the job well.

There is some bias here which needs to be reformed.

Our laws limit the number and qualifications of expatriates but they are easily circumvented due to poor monitoring by our bureaucracy.

Trade inequity

In the matter of exports, we export basic raw materials to you, leaving a very small room for us to process them.

You then export back to us, at much higher value, goods processed from the raw materials we sent.

As a result, there is no balance of trade. We should strive for an equitable trade
balance.

Hasty tourism advisories

Regarding tourism, considering that our fledgling tourism industry is still largely dependent on tourists coming from Japan, the impact of travel advisories from your government discouraging Japanese citizens from visiting our country can easily be imagined.

A recent case is the advisory issued in the wake of the kidnapping here in the Philippines of Mr. Wakaoji, a Japanese executive.

As it turned out later after Mr. Wakaoji was rescued, the alleged/rumored kidnappers were not only Filipino criminals; rather, there were some Japanese members of the Yakuza syndicate.

Due to the advisory to drop the Philippines as a tourist destination, the damage to the Philippine tourism industry was tremendous.

Millions of potential tourist dollars were lost as Japanese citizens cancelled their planned visits to our country. Perhaps a more careful, and less hasty, process of issuing advisories would be of greater mutual benefit to both countries.

Visa ordeal

For Japanese who come here, we lay out the red carpet and require no visas. But for Filipinos who want to go to Japan, we have to queue up under the sun for two to three hours, even more, outside the Japanese visa office. Thus, every Filipino who gets his or her visa after such an ordeal already feels great resentment even before he has set foot on Japanese soil.

I wonder, perhaps, where diplomatic channels fail, the powerful *Keidan-ren* can help us get our visas with dignity and reciprocal civility?

Right investors needed

I know I have said things which may not have been very pleasant to hear. But I say these things based on facts and common sense with the purpose of building a stronger and happier relationship. As hard-nosed business executives, I trust you will appreciate some friendly advocacy that will bind us closer.

While the truth may discourage some investors from coming in, chances are such investors are the wrong kind of investors, anyway. The kind who are concerned only with making a quick profit for themselves
with no regard for the development of the Filipino nation, so it can finally lift itself out of massive poverty.

My hope is that the truth will encourage the right kind of investors to come in, the kind of investors genuinely interested in mutual benefit for themselves and the nation hosting them.

VII
Pushing Exports Means Commitment to Export Growth *(Not Revenue Generation and More Regulations)*

Assembly of the Philippine Exporters Foundation, Inc.; 1990

Exports: First priority?

A year ago, President Corazon Aquino at our First Exporters' Conference said: "I want to make it clear and categorical: exports will be given the highest national priority today."

Because of this commitment, President Aquino designated the DTI (Department of Trade and Industry) as lead government agency in spurring efforts by cutting government red tape. She also set a 72-hour deadline for DTI to respond to the expressed needs of exporters.

It has been one year since that convention. And, although we believe in the sincerity of the President in pushing exports and in the industriousness of our colleagues in government, the sad truth is that the Philippines still lags behind its ASEAN brothers in export performance.

Contradictory positions

I think part of the reason is the frequently contradictory relationship between government and private sector.

One party wants to tackle the conflicting issues with the goal of achieving a solution that is really export growth led and not bureaucratic and revenue-oriented. On the other hand, while government wishes to make exports a priority concern yet, either in the implementation or in the structural rules, the private sector perceives the government to be more committed to generating revenue than to accelerating and sustaining growth of exports.

Philippines, Inc.: Push national interests abroad

Developing our exports means that we in the private sector must band together with our colleagues in government and create a Philippines, Inc. - a mindset, as it were, of pushing Filipino interests first in the international marketplace. That is the mindset that will propel Philippine exports past our international rivals, the kind of mindset in our government colleagues that will convince us that exports are, indeed, a high national priority.

Protect our non-competitive products

Having this mindset means being convinced of this truism: Pushing exports means cutting down all barriers, both tariff and non-tariff, for products that the Philippines has an advantage and not for those that will further marginalize our non-competitive products.

I believe that when President Aquino said "I want to make it clear and categorical: exports will be given the highest priority today, I give the Department of Trade and Industry (DTI) a 72-hour deadline to respond to the needs of exporters," she was making more of a political statement than a policy statement.

Who would believe that the DTI can perform this miracle? It has been years and years that the exporters have been crying out their immediate needs first just to survive in their export business not to mention rival our foreign competitors.

Multinationals favored?

After survival, exporters want sustainable growth. Every export sector has submitted all sorts of position papers, attended many meetings, and only a trickle has been addressed. Nowhere is it in sight that our exporters will be growing and sustained, except for those products like the semi-conductor exports owned by multinationals for processing, assembly to their mother companies in US, Japan, Korea, Taiwan, and the like. On this specific issue, all red tape and bureaucracy have been totally removed and their components were whisked through the ports 24 hours a day and whisked out in the same manner.

I have no objection to this kind of bold action to address the concerns of multinational companies of avoiding delay in their exports. My only concern is the selective procedure for a few with powerful clout as against the majority of other exporters with voices of little clout.

How about small exporters?

Among the voices with little clout are the agri-aqua farmers who suffer from the following problems:

- Poor and very expensive transportation facilities to bring their products to the ports;
- Absence of roads, water, electricity, communication in their areas thus compounding not only costs but subjecting their produce to deterioration and destruction;
- Lack of government support on management, technology, extension services (if any is given, it is hardly sufficient);
- Reluctance of banking institutions to give rural credit for these operations; banks usually give credit only to big companies with good track record or with collateral assets, leaving the small, medium agri-aqua farmers to borrow from loan sharks at high interest rates;
- Land distributed to the farmers as the centerpiece of Aquino's Administration is a political and non- sustainable policy as many of these otherwise productive lands became non-productive due to lack or absence of support to the farmers. Many resold their lands. A few exceptions may have some small successes but with minimal national impact hardly called a worthy and credible achievement.

Needed: Equal treatment of multinationals and Filipino exporters

What the government has done for the multinational companies which co-export semi-conductors should likewise have been made available to the Filipino exporters in sectors similarly situated as the multinationals. Then this would be a good sign to test sincerity of the government in pushing exports for all.

Avoid favoring certain sectors

At this point, I cite also the danger of favoring one sector of exporters to the disadvantage of others.

Every export sector is an important cog in the wheel and a breakdown on the semi-conductor cog could be adding more difficulties such as displacement of jobs and foreign exchange revenues (even though the net forex is very much less than the gross revenue used in their measurement of export growth).

In the future as the focus of business shifts, it may be possible that many of these multinational semi-conductor exports will transfer to other regions with less labor cost and better infrastructure and incentives.

Therefore, I submit that government should work with the private sector more actively, more responsively, and more candidly, and avoid mere lip-service and rhetoric.

Cut red tape

I cannot go into specifics but even in the area of bureaucracy, we need less paperwork, less lost time in processing requirements, less layering of unnecessary signatures or initials, or even less people to deal with. The axiom "less is more" has never been truer than in our maze of bureaucratic processes.

Let us work towards a mindset of Philippines, Inc., where all converge on the target of making Philippine interest as the center point. To trust in our own people and work for their common good.

Mabuhay ang Pilipino!

VIII
Export Business: Experiences and Lessons

Paper delivered as Guest Lecturer to Master of Business Management (MBM) students of the Asian Institute of Management (AIM), Makati City;
August 31, 1993

Export, as a subject, is close to my heart because of the many valuable lessons in life I have learned from my exporting experience.

I have experienced disappointments, renewed energy and hope. I consider rejections of my products by export buyers as only temporary setbacks and not outright failures. I always hope that with some improvement, the product I offer will eventually be in agreement with my buyer.

More importantly, I believe, the export business has taught me a lot of lessons about the world and about people. And this continuous interaction has encouraged me to continue improving and to continue learning.

Learning from mistakes

However, my experience in the export world was at the start a failure. This was the initial export of shrimps to Japan in 1973 to 1975.

At about the same time, in 1974 to 1977, I tried to export Sony TV monitors to various overseas markets upon Sony-Japan's job orders. This, too, was a calamity.

In both instances, I lost money. It humbled me. But I gained experience and improved my outlook. It taught me valuable lessons. In the end, the experience proved to be rewarding and fulfilling.

Since then, I have been actively involved in exporting various products to the global market. After those initial years of failure to sell shrimps to Japan, our company was finally able to break into the Japanese market. We eventually pioneered in the export of black tiger prawns and processed crab meat to Japan and the United States, respectively.

We are also exporting black and white television sets, colored television sets, radio cassette recorders, car radios, and even Kia cars in SKD form to Vietnam.

We are currently in the production planning stage for the export of color television sets to Europe which uses a different broadcast system than ours - the PAL/ SECAM system. We are looking at a total export to Europe of 1,000,000 TV sets by next year.

Aside from being active in the export business, I have spent seven years in helping an export foundation, which was in the red at the time I became its president. Together with idealistic and sincere colleagues in the board, we nurtured it to make it an asset-healthy organization that today has cash strength of over a hundred million pesos.

Exports good for local economy

To me, export is both balm and boon to a country's well-being.

Exports create employment and incomes which the domestic market alone could not do. Exports, in fact, revitalize the domestic market as it enlarges the size of the domestic market to the extent that higher incomes and more jobs are created.

Exports result to more rapid innovation and emulation among exporting firms as they respond to a larger and more exacting clientele. Exporters learn to become more efficient to achieve lower unit cost in order to become price-competitive. The efficiency of operations and upgrading are imperatives for survival when producing for the world market.

Exports earn hard currency and thus contribute to the country's pool of foreign exchange receipts. It can be said therefore that exporting industries "pay for their own way" as well as for imports of other industries.

One reason why we borrowed so heavily in the past was that our exports lagged so badly that we were not earning enough hard currency to pay for our import requirements.

Export ethos: Anti-corruption tool

Finally, but more importantly, I think, the effect of an "export ethos" on our society and country will have the effect of reducing corruption because of the need to compete and be efficient in the world markets.

Show me a nation that has not prospered by its strong exports. Just look around us in our own backyard and the answer smacks right into our faces.

Japan: Building from ashes

Japan was a totally devastated country after World War II. She not only had to rebuild the lives of her people from the ashes of war but each Japanese had to work to pay war reparations and damages to many countries she injured. Despite this double whammy, her leadership mustered the will and the courage to overcome a national disgrace and inspired the Japanese people to a mission of hard work, humility, austerity and sacrifice for love of country and the honor of their people.

With pride in their hearts, the Japanese people innovated and produced high quality products that met global acceptance. Denying themselves comfort and physical convenience, they united, harmonized, and helped one another and moved as a people to overcome pain and difficulties. They did not bicker, fight, grandstand, point fingers of blame at one another, or abuse their position. Their goal was, first and foremost, national prosperity. They rallied under the cry "growth and export expansion," which was further clarified under the interlocking triad of "growth, investment, and exports."

Japan, Inc., was the unifying force.

Today, Japan is the strongest economic power in Asia and is challenging the United States and Europe in product excellence in every field.

Other Asian dragons

Every other country that excelled has shown tremendous export growth. Korea, Taiwan, Hong Kong, Singapore, and now China are shining examples of Asian dragons who have exhibited fine performance in their exports.

In tandem with export growth, their GNP increased, their employment and technological enhancement multiplied, their foreign exchange reserves grew by leaps and bounds, and most of all their pride and national consciousness bonded them into great nations worthy of world recognition and admiration.

During this decade of the nineties, we see Thailand, Malaysia and Indonesia inching up and surfacing to become new Asian dragons.

I do not have to bore you with statistics that show that in the sixties up to the mid-seventies, the Philippines was way ahead of all in Asia, playing second only to Japan.

Today, we find ourselves sliding backward in many areas while our ASEAN neighbors are carving out their special niches in their domestic and global victories.

The Philippine performance: Post-World War II

Where are we today?

From the time the Americans liberated the Philippines from the Japanese occupation forces in World War II to today is about half a century.

After half a century, majority of the Filipino people are still deeply mired in poverty. **We are still highly dependent on imported goods even for the simplest products. We still have almost zero manufacturing capability.**

While our Asian neighbors, such as South **Korea and Malaysia, proudly manufacture and export cars and other industrial products, there is still no such thing as even a Philippine-made motorcycle or bicycle.** What is the onus of this failure to bring about economic growth and prosperity for our people?

Rights without responsibilities

One factor is our Constitution. The four post-war constitutions that we have had, including the present one, have emphasized rights but not responsibilities. As a result, we take no serious responsibility for economic development, but we demand our right to be.

Flip-flopping policies destroy credibility

All through these years, the government has had flip-flopping policies which have resulted to lack of credibility.

This condition has discouraged the growth of direct foreign investments and thus has limited the infusion of capital and technology into the country. Even domestic investors take a "wait-and-see" attitude since government's policies seem to have neither rhyme nor reason and influence- peddling seems to be the order of the day.

The rule of law is mouthed but not practiced. Where else can we find a situation where the public perception of government is contemptuous?

There is more distrust than respect for public officials. Hoodlums in uniform, in robes, in Congress, in business suits (monopolists, cartels, behest loan beneficiaries, etc.)

Characteristics of inconsistency

This inconsistency and instability in government policies has been characterized by:

- Aping American way of life and policy (loose democracy unsuitable to the Asian way of life; implementation of the due process and equal protection clauses in the constitution);
- Restrictions/regulations calculated to benefit a few and grounds for corruption and graft;
- Monopolistic and cartelized economy;
- Special franchise and protection of local industries enjoyed by a few;
- - Smuggling;
- Corruption, bribery, greed;
- Political dynasties;
- "Open-close-open" foreign exchange policy
- Elitism in government bureaucracy - "Mr. Know-it-all" is it. Does not listen;
- Waste, neglect, hypocrisy
- Insensitivity to reforms, immorality.

These have resulted in severe political and economic distortions which have wrought havoc in the national soul and dignity of the Filipino.

Change: Find new and better ways

You may wonder why I am presenting these things to you.

For the Filipinos who are the members of this class, I want you to be sensitive to the real issues that really matter.

When you go out of this elite institution of learning, I want you to think not only of maximizing profits and the bottom line, but also to take a macro view of our country and people.

Do not merely follow the ways of the old generation. Contribute to make a change in our country that will bring about prosperity and happiness for our people.

Your new report card should be unlike the one that I showed you earlier.

And because you are still young, time is with you and you can definitely make a difference!

And yes, let us export quality goods and services. And also goodwill.

For the non-Filipino members of this class, now that you have taken a glimpse of our weaknesses, I hope that when you go back to your own countries and occupy positions of power, you might remember this talk today and think not of exploiting the Philippines and the Filipinos.

Grab opportunities

I would not want to disappoint you today. You invited me to talk to you about export opportunities and pitfalls.

Spotting business opportunities, let alone export business opportunities, is something that is difficult to teach in school. One has to be in business to be able to recognize these opportunities. It is one thing to push figures and come out with nice projections, and another thing to really do the actual transactions. Nevertheless, I shall try my best to share with you some of my experience with the hope that you may be able to profit from it.

One skill that you will find valuable is how to grab and make use of opportunities or sudden streaks of good luck. Serendipity, I think, can be found in almost all histories of successful companies.

Day 1: No shrimps

The idea for exporting prawns to Japan, for example, came to me when I was worrying about what to do with a piece of idle land in Tondo. And then, in a function I attended, I was served succulent prawns. I complimented my host who told me that the prawns had been locally processed and frozen fresh so I thought: Why not use my land for processing shrimps? But I found out that it was not as easy as that.

We went through many trying years before we even began seeing break-even results. My son-in-law, who is running our agri-business operations, likes to tell the story of how he and one of our plant managers waited and waited for their first batch of prawns to process in Roxas City.

It was 1979. Day 1 came and went: No Shrimps. On Day 2, as they were watching everyone pass them by, a tricycle stopped in front of them. Out came a man with a pail of fresh shrimps. And that's how we started our processing operations in that city.

But the difficult time was yet to come. You see, at first, the Japanese did not find the Black Tiger prawn acceptable, mainly because of its black sheen. So we went all out with a marketing blitz to convince the Japanese dealers to consider our product. We invited some of them into the country to see our plants. Then we took to the Japanese marketplaces ourselves and cooked the prawns right before their very eyes. The cooking process, of course, turned the black tiger prawns into mouth-watering and sumptuous red delicacies.

To make a long story short, after a couple of years of failure and successive losses, we were finally able to convince the Japanese that our fresh frozen black tiger prawns were one of the best in the world. From there, we set about in establishing a reputation for excellent quality and price- competitive products.

Consumer electronics export: Not on silver platter

The opportunity to export consumer electronic products was an offshoot of our relationship with Sony Corporation of Japan. But such an opportunity did not come on a silver platter. We had to work hard for it.

We first had to convince the Japanese that our production systems and quality of our output were up to their exacting standards. Sony tested us in the domestic market.

You see, our company is the only licensed Sony manufacturer in the whole world where Sony has no equity interest or Sony managers. After we had proven to the Japanese that we could produce quality products, it was only then that Sony gave us the opportunity to export some of our products bearing the Sony name to some of their global customers.

The opportunity to export color TV to Europe is a result of changing trade conditions in the world marketplace. Malaysia, Thailand and Singapore used to be the largest suppliers of this product. However, due to changing tariff rules, these countries are now unable to supply Europe with this product at preferential tariff rates. Our excellent manufacturing capability, honed by our long years of experience in producing high quality Sony products, will enable us to take advantage of this opportunity given the fact that the Philippine is qualified for GSP to Europe.

You can't plan opportunities

One cannot plan or program business opportunities. In some instances, we have picked up what were thought of as discards of other companies and converted them into viable opportunities.

The following are a few examples: Sony

When Sony first came to the Philippines, we were not its first distributor. That distinction was given to another Filipino business group which came out with a line of audio products called "Sony-Elitone." They held the Sony franchise for five years until, inexplicably, they gave it up. Perhaps, they did not see the potentials of the business. That was how we came to pick up the Sony manufacturing, distribution, and servicing franchise in the Philippines.

Prawn

Our prawn processing plant in Roxas City was originally a boarded-up plant of the Shrimp Corporation of the Philippines. We picked it up, rehabilitated and refurbished it, and now it is one of the most productive processing plants of our agribusiness group.

Tristar

Tristar, our black and white picture tube factory, is currently occupying buildings vacated by Magma Rubber Corporation. We put in the assembly lines, the baking, lacquering and related equipment, and Tristar has since gone on to become the market leader in the black and white picture tube manufacturing in the Philippines.

Industrial estate

Our industrial estate project in Binan, Laguna is also a discard, albeit a political one.

You see, the land which we developed as an industrial estate was rumored to be owned by the late President Marcos.

It was surrendered to the government by one of his cronies, and the government in turn distributed the land to the farmers.

We bought the land from a farmers' cooperative which acted in behalf of the farmers. Now, we have built a productive industrial estate which will have more than fifty companies which will employ about 125,000 direct and indirect workers.

What once was an unproductive, barren land is now going to provide employment opportunities and export revenues to Filipinos.

People's Car

Our People's Car business can also be classified as the result of a product line which had been discarded by other car manufacturing companies. Mitsubishi, Toyota, and Volkswagen all had small-car entries in the market which they subsequently discontinued because of very thin margins. We made the People's car a necessity in many homes and businesses. Our factory site and head office were leftovers from what was once the Delta Motors Group. We bought the properties through public auction and breathed new life into them. Today, these properties have once more become productive.

Opportunities everywhere

What do these mean? There are opportunities everywhere. The lowly discard could prove to be a highly successful venture with the right vision.

Promoting our prawn export business has even introduced me to more business opportunities.

Four years ago, I was part of a Philippine trade mission to Europe. My role was to sell our prawns to the Europeans. Well, that's exactly what I did. I cornered a Belgian delegate and regaled him with my best spiel on prawns. After I finished my sales pitch, he looked at me and said: "But Madame, I'm not interested in your prawns. I am about to try to convince you to be the exclusive distributor of our trucks and buses in the Philippines." But that is another story.

Three steps to success

Truly, the whole world is out there waiting to be conquered, but one has to be able to ride out the waves of setbacks that will inevitably come your way.

To keep afloat, there are two basic things that you have to think about: price and quality.

But how do you deliver excellent quality and at the same time be price-competitive?

Know your product well

First, it is imperative that you know your product well - from raw materials to processing to finishing.

There is absolutely no shortcut to achieve this.

You cannot start any business with you sitting behind a large desk and accepting orders immediately.   .

Step 1 involves rolling up your sleeves arid knowing what you have.

Attainable targets

Step 2 means setting your sights on targets within reach.

We have often been told to think big. Well, we started our prawn business with only a hundred-thousand pesos.

If you are just starting in exports, try going small-scale first. That will give you more time to organize your business as well as to identify your niche. By the time the larger orders come in, you will be better prepared and your support systems will already be in place.

Speculations? I would not advise it even if you have already gained some experience. Why risk dislocation when careful planning may eventually yield the same results.

Good team

Step 3 is developing a team that will not lose sight of your original objective: High Quality Products at Competitive Prices. You must invest in your people through training. You must also instill in them the right values as much as you see to it that they are justly treated. Your team must love your product as much as you do - but you must have respect for your people, too.

Quality top priority

After that, it is time to learn riding the waves. But never forget that quality is the top priority in conquering the export market. I think our experience has shown that those who are hardest hit during bad times are those who have taken too many shortcuts and are contented with substandard products. But foreign buyers will not take any risk. They will always go to the producer that will give them quality goods each time.

Corollary to this is the assurance of continuity of supply, no matter what. You cannot ask the dealers to stop selling even during difficult times. More than ever, they need to be assured that you will have what they need when they need it. You must deliver whatever you commit. Dependability, in other words, is high in the list of priorities in the export market.

But dependability as an export producer is not the same as predictability.

Customer not always right

Your customers' standards of quality will not always be constant. The specifications of one market may not be the same as another. You will have to be flexible: If your customers demand changes, you must be quick to adjust and adapt to changing market conditions.

But while your customers would be the final judge of your products, think twice if fulfilling their wishes would extract too much from you.

That is why continuous research and development is very important to exports: So that you will always have a ready substitute for something that your customers suddenly find unacceptable.

I have tried to put many cautionary notes in this talk simply because going into exports is fraught with danger. The export market is not for the faint of heart.

Other forms of profit

As I referred to earlier in my talk, profits from export should not be seen solely in financial terms. Introducing new technology to our country is a profit. Providing our people with thousands of job opportunities is a profit. But these profits do not go into our company's income statement. Yet they go a long way in feeding our national soul. And they are earned only when there is sincere concern and conviction to contribute positively to the collective spirit instead of concentrating only on one's own wellbeing.

The Philippine Report Card that I showed you earlier shows that our country has had more than its fair share of bad luck and economic mismanagement for the past half century. But we should try to move on. Business should influence the thinking and direct the policies of government.

Filipino First

Whenever we fight our way through in the export market, always remember who we are: Filipinos. Our performance abroad reflects not only our employees but on our country and fellow Filipinos.

We, Filipinos, should be the first to have faith in our own abilities. Only after that can we ask our foreign friends who are here with us today and even those who are not here to have faith in the Filipino and in his works.   ,

In our company, this Filipino-ness is ingrained in our corporate culture such that part of our corporate credo goes like this:

We believe in the Filipino.

We must prove the Filipino s worth by making products that compete in the world markets, by striving to include Philippine-made components in our products, and by making use of Filipino ingenuity and capability.

You may want to think about this whenever you start losing faith in ourselves or hope in our country.

Thank you.

IX
We Must Have Faith in The Filipino, Our Selves

Opening Session of the Corporate Planning Meeting of MCCI Corporation;
September 7, 1993

Ladies and Gentlemen: Thank you very much for your gracious invitation. I feel honored in addressing a group of talented Filipino managers working for an all-Filipino corporation such as MCCI. It is doubly pleasurable for me because the topic at hand is something which is very close to my heart - that of investing in our beloved country.

It has become very fashionable nowadays to engage in Philippine-bashing. And for obvious reasons - it seems that every conceivable disaster has happened to the Philippines for the last two decades.

Challenges We Must Face

Indeed, why should businessmen invest in the Philippines?

Even a cursory look at the country's economic progress since Independence Day on July 4, 1946, will reveal that the Philippines is indeed the "sick man of Asia." This malaise became much more pronounced in the past decade - most notably in trade and investment.

The area of exports, for example is where we performed particularly badly vis-a-vis our Southeast Asian neighbors. While they chalked up phenomenal export growth rates of more than 30% from the 1970s onwards, our annual export growth rate has remained at a measly 18%.

I prepared a report card of the Philippine economy for a talk I recently gave to students of the Asian Institute of Management, and this I also want to show you. In this report card, we can see that although the Philippines has been independent for almost fifty years, no real economic progress has been made.

Our GNP is at a very poor $48.93 billion while our per capita GNP figure of $760 is not even 50% of what it takes to qualify our country for inclusion in the exclusive club of newly industrializing countries.

Our government projects that the country will reach this level by the end of this century - thus the slogan Philippines 2000. However, if we look at the measly GNP growth rate of *0.62%,* then we will realize the huge gap between the grand dream and sobering reality.

I stated earlier that our Philippine export performance was particularly bad. The picture would become worse if we juxtapose this performance against imports worth $14.48 billion. This would result in a balance of trade deficit of $4,671 billion.

Such poor economic indicators would naturally spur any thinking government into belt-tightening measures. But so far: this government has not gone into that. Our government bureaucracy still stands at 1.9 million employees, around 1.2 million of whom are in "plantilla" or regular positions. To say that the government bureau-cracy is bloated is a big understatement - especially if we consider that government workers represent 11% of the total Philippine workforce.

Admittedly, the private sector has not provided enough jobs. Our nationwide unemployment rate hovers around 10%, this despite the number of contract workers we keep on sending overseas.

Other Issues

But we businessmen have a lot of causes to complain. Why invest in the Philippines if the crime rate is soaring? Why invest if corruption in government undermines even the most legitimate of ventures?

Add these concerns to the frequent power outages, for which we pay in rates which are reputedly one of the highest in Asia. Add also the lack of infrastructure, the lack of telecommunication facilities, the lack of water, the lack of housing, and we will indeed conclude that the Philippines has a long way to go before it can consider itself a newly industrializing country.

And the majority of the Filipino people seems to agree with these sentiments. In recent surveys conducted by the Social Weather Stations, the executive, the legislative, and judicial branches of the government got extremely low ratings - with the judicial branch bringing up the rear.

It seems only the controversial Health Secretary Juan Flavier is doing a good job, according to the perception of the people.

Faith in the Filipino

Faced with all these negative data, what message can we gather?

If one focuses only on numbers and rationality, then one will conclude that the Philippines is not a good country to invest in. To this sort of person, even a communist country like Vietnam will be a better alternative to the Philippines. However, I am not a person who focuses only on numbers, trends, and rational analysis. I would not be speaking to you today if I only believed in these things.

I am the sort of person who sees problems and does something to solve them. I am not the sort of person who analyzes problem to death and gets paralyzed by their sheer complexity.

Our prawn-processing company, AA Export & Import Corp., is an extension of this sort of thinking. Although it is now the dominant leader in the Philippine prawn export industry, AA EXICO encountered a lot of difficulties before it opened the Japan market for black tiger prawns. You see, the Japanese hated the black tiger prawn because of its color. If we had been overcome by first impression, we would have given up and maybe this unknown specie of prawn would have remained in our brackish ponds. To overcome this bias, I had to personally go to Japan and demonstrate that the black tiger, when cooked, would turn into a deliciously reddish color. Two years of hard work, promotion and goodwill made the black tiger prawn finally an acceptable export commodity to Japan.

Another example: In 1984, when our economy was in shambles

and Jobo bills of the Central Bank were being peddled at 45% interest, I decided to put up a P20 million prawn processing plant in Bacolod, when nobody (had faith in Negros Occidental Province due to the collapse of the sugar industry. I patiently waited for two years before any prawns from our growers could be processed to serve as start-up production for our plant. Inspired by our vision, the Negrenses rose again and prawn export industry became the industry that it is today. You ask what factors determine my decisions regarding investments? The first is faith. Yes, faith in the Philippines and the Filipino.

As I stated before, if one concentrates only on the negative things, then one will be so utterly discouraged that one will not move. We all have to have faith - and this cannot be gotten merely by looking at numbers.

This Filipino nationalism also propels us to localize raw materials for our finished products, especially electronics. We want to prove that local businesses can compete with world-class giants. _

Serve our people

The second factor which determines our investments is the opportunity to provide genuine service to our people. By nature, I am a problem-solver. The companies I have set up, therefore, are all pro-posed solutions to problems — problems that spring from the legitimate needs of our people for a better life. The Solid Group of Companies is into basic or near-basic products and services: communication, food processing, land development, transportation - the very sparkplugs to fire up the country's engine to progress.

An example of this resolve can be found in our car company, Columbian Autocar Corporation.

I went into this in the first place because I felt that Filipinos deserve a less expensive mode of transportation than what was then being offered at the time by the three big Japanese-led car manufacturers.

We introduced the Kia Pride, the first ever People's Car brand in the market. Until then only three Japanese car brands could be seen on the streets. I saw the unfairness of this and challenged the government to change its policy. It took 18 months to fight for this cause before change finally came. But change did come and I thank God for using me as his instrument to effect the change of the policy for the good of the Filipino consumers.

Opportunities in crisis

The third factor determining our investments is that we look at opportunities where others see only crisis.

The People's Car is an example - this was a product line discarded by the Japanese car makers which we resurrected.

Another example is Solid Corporation, one of our oldest companies which is better known as the franchise holder of Sony Corporation in the Philippines.

We did not start out this way. When Sony first came to the Philippines, we were not its first distributor. That distinction was given to another Filipino business group, which came out with a line of audio products called Sony-Elitone. They held the Sony franchise for five years until, inexplicably, they gave it up. Perhaps they did not see the potential in this business. That was how we came to pick up the Sony manufacturing, distribution, and servicing franchise in the Philippines.   .

Why am I telling you this? The moral is that there are opportunities everywhere. But in order to see these opportunities clearly, one must have faith, vision, and the courage to pursue these opportunities - sometimes despite what the numbers say.

Creative rather than analytical

Corporate planning sessions such as this one call on managers to analyze a lot of macroeconomic and business-related data. That is fine.

However, we must never forget that the inspired strategic thinker is creative rather than analytical. He must be driven by a vision to solve problems not only for the sake of profit for the company but for a higher ideal. This is what differentiates the mere numbers-cruncher from the real business-builder.

Be cathedral-builders

I am reminded of a story about the three workers who were involved in the building of a cathedral in Rheims, France a long time ago. The building was still in its initial stages when a passer-by inquired from the three what they were doing. The first worker answered that he was merely putting stones together. The second worker replied that he was putting up a wall. The third worker said, while gazing dreamily upwards, that he was helping make a cathedral.

Be cathedral-builders, then. Think creatively and look for opportunities whefe others fear to tread. This is the attitude which builds strong businesses. And this is the attitude that will also make the Philippines a better- place to invest in.

Thank you. very much.

X
CICC: Moving Towards a New Strategic Alliance for the 21st Century

Customs-Industry Consultative Council (CICC), 8th Anniversary; (1995)

Love-hate relationship

February 5,1995, saw the dawning of a new chapter in Philippine Economic History - the institutionalization of an alliance between the Business Community and the Bureau of Customs via the establishment of the "Customs-Industry Consultative Council (CICC)."

This NGO (non-governmental organization) was designed primarily to serve as the forum for the Customs and Industry dialogue, ventilation of conflicts and the advancement of developmental collaboration and the partnership for a progressive Philippines.

CICC was indeed conceptualized ahead of its time. As we recall in the past, the traditional relationship between Customs and Industry has often been adversarial and confrontational, truly a love-hate relationship.

"Perestroika"

But this pioneering policy has changed all that. The door opened a new era and has sown the seeds of a new global thinking that was first fertilized in Philippine soil. Thus, what followed was a period of openness, cooperation, coordination, communication and consultation which ushered in our own version of *"Glasnost"* (openness) and ultimately led to the start of the BOC *"Perestroika"* (restructuring).

This regular contact and intercourse of ideas between Customs and Industry leaders started the RE-VISIONING of the BOC's role in society. For a while, the industry's intense advocacy for government sensitivity towards the need of the private sector has led to a major refocusing from an overprotective and enforcement-oriented agency into a pro-people and stakeholder- oriented service agency.

CICC Accomplishments

The major accomplishments of the CICC are the elimination of red-tape, bureaucratic maze, the eradication of graft and corruption in all levels and the promotion of effectiveness and efficiency in public service.

Most important of all is the joint formulation of policies embodied in the Customs Memorandum Orders (CMOs) that served as a guide for the whole industry. Yet, we cannot rest on our laurels because we know this period is just short-lived due to changes in administration and the interplay of politics from within and without.

As the CICC looks into its future, we look back momentarily and reflect on the original vision and mission of the organization as we ponder over an excerpt from the speech of the former President Corazon Aquino delivered during the inauguration of the CICC and I quote -

"I welcome the creation of the Customs-Industry Consultative Council. The first responsibility of the Bureau is to serve the country s traders and to promote the growth of our industries. We cannot collect duties and taxes if the businessmen are not making profits. We cannot squeeze juice from a turnip.

"I am sure our businessmen will be more than happy to pay taxes to government if they are making money.

"The leaders of the business community should take an active interest in Customs affairs and conduct constant dialogue with its officials and employees. The Consultative Council can serve as forum for this.

"Our traders shall formulate policies and recommend measures which will expedite these transactions with the Bureau.

"They have every right to demand prompt and efficient service from our Customs officials and employees. After all, they are the Customers and they provide income to finance the operations of our government.

"The Bureau must promote rather than hamper the growth of commerce and industry. .

"Regulations and rules are formulated for the purpose of ensuring the orderly conduct of business and for reconciling the interests of all concerned.

"Protecting the higher interest of our people and our government is not the monopoly of those in public service. Most of the true patriots are in the private sector, not in government."

For several years now, the CICC has been in interregnum. Our time was spent in thorough introspection of where the organization is headed. And as we contemplate and look around us, we were amazed to discover a major development on the rise among the Customs Administrations in the Asia-Pacific Region. A re-engineering movement has started and the catalyst to this phenomenon was the collaboration between Customs and Industry, exactly the very same concept that we had implemented eight years ago in the Philippines.

Lessons from other countries

As we look closer, we are overwhelmed to learn that the industry groups in the region are not consultative organizations but monitoring and advisory arms of the top leaders of government (ministerial level) and the composition of the industry group is created by the passage of law.

One of the leading lights of these partnerships is Australia's "Customs Advisory Board," tasked to make independent and regular reports on the reforms being implemented in government. The Minister receives their evaluation reports and acts on their recommendations when necessary.

A much bolder group is USA's "Joint Industry Group (JIG)," a coalition of more than a hundred companies, trade associations and businesses actively involved in international trade. They are presently involved in the drafting of legislative reforms for Customs, review of international agreements, and the designing of Cargo Clearance Processes, but as the world marches on we cannot but wonder on our present predicament and be awakened by the reality that we cannot be just spectators to this historic period.

It shouldn't matter if the present dispensation is not receptive to the ideas of industry. We should start moving ahead, get our act together and launch a massive industry initiated program for the Bureau of Customs.

CICC's vision of a world-class customs service is embodied in its eight-point reform program for a BOC for the next century, specifically:

TOTAL QUALITY MANAGEMENT - Re-engineering examines work processes according to value-addedness, testing each step in the work process to ensure that it adds value from the Customers' perspective and designs in quality. Re-engineering uses much of the external customer focus and internal processes compliance and quality measurement as baseline to measure progress and set strength objectives.

PARTICIPATORY MANAGEMENT - Shifting of work emphasis to teams that function horizontally and communicate directly with each other with minimal supervision thus requiring higher levels of workforce cooperation and worker development.

STRATEGIC PLANNING - Re-engineering seeks to identify the most critical operational process of the organization, to realign these work process to exceed current and bridge future customer requirements and market needs and to re-invest change resources and supporting technology to these priorities.

PROCESS MANAGEMENT - Shifting of the management emphasis from highly specialized functions to process management so that work can be done parallel, not in set function thus reducing cycle time and minimizing hands-off work transfer from supplier and across internal organizational boundaries.

COMPLIANCE MEASUREMENT - Performance evaluation is a way of gauging the effectiveness of our initiatives and efforts.

LEGISLATIVE RESTRUCTURING - The business community should be given the opportunity to review and propose laws that will equally favor the interest of government and industry.

EDUCATION - Customs and Industry have to join hands in helping educate the business community as the requirement of Customs compliance.

GLOBALIZATION - Industry must assist Customs in helping it achieve the highest degree of simplification and harmonization of Customs Systems and procedures and to make it at par with international Standards by way of active involvement in international Conferences such as the World Customs Organization (WCO), United Nations Conference on Trade and Development (UNCTAD), Asia Pacific Economic Cooperation (APEC), ASEAN Free Trade (AFTA) and others.

The private sector must learn that the entire reengineering cycle, from vision to planning to redesign, to conversion to implementation, may take several years, but many benefits, the so-called deliverables, can be realized as we go through the process.   ,

Finally, the paramount goal of the CICC is to achieve the delivery of government service that is equal to the best in the business. To deliver the level of quality that Filipinos will enjoy. This revolutionary step will ultimately be a major step towards the restoration of confidence in government service.

XI The Filipino in Global Competition

8th National Convention, Production Management Association of the Philippines, Subic Freeport Zone,
Olongapo City, September 22, 1995

Best and worst

"It was the best of times. It was the worst of times." Thus did the English author Charles Dickens begin his famous novel, "A Tale of Two Cities."

The two cities Dickens was referring to were, of course, London and Paris in the 1800s - two cities reaping the early fruits of the industrial revolution but being tom apart by social and political strife.

The best of times and the worst of times.

These words could also describe the Philippines in 1995 - a Philippines that is on the verge of economic recovery, but being sorely tested by rampant criminality and political infighting. Yes, we are experiencing growth in almost all market sectors in the Philippines, but global competitors are also coming in and grabbing a share of this increased market.

The banking sector, for instance, will see the increased competition not only from the likes of Chase Manhattan but also from Dao Heng of Hongkong and Bangkok Bank of Thailand. The retail sector, long protected by the Philippine Constitution, will also see increased competition as giant international players like Makro of the Netherlands come into the scene.

The best of times, and the worst of times.

There is a poster I remember seeing long ago which perhaps describes the feeling of Filipino businessmen: "Just when I thought I knew all the answers, they changed all the questions."
Ready?

Just when the economy is finally moving and getting interesting, arid local companies are finally getting their acts together, the government opens up the arena and global players start moving in. Are we really ready for this?

The question is rhetorical, of course,
because whether local businessmen are ready or not, these global players will come in. Rather than bewailing the increased competition in our local markets, we local businessmen should think about getting our costs in line and getting product quality up to par so that consumers will still patronize our products. We should also be thinking about expanding our horizons through exports that we can get the volumes we need to get our unit costs down and hone our quality to international standards.

Not just money

There is this easy temptation, once you get to a certain level of financial security, just to take it easy. People constantly tell me: "Use your money to make more money. Play with stocks and bonds. That way, you will have less headaches and end up with better returns." This is well-meaning advice from well-meaning people, and I readily thank these people for their concern. But I think they miss the point.

I am not in business merely for the money.

My joy is in seeing products roll out from an assembly line, ready for shipping to consumers who are eager to buy. I like to see capital produce tangible products - products that people can hold, play with, and enjoy.

My joy is in being able to provide Filipinos with decent jobs in order to help their families grow. My joy is in seeing Filipinos growing in their jobs, and helping their companies compete with formidable foreign opponents. That is why I continually exhort my managers and employees: Do not for one second believe that foreigners are better than you! If they can do it, we can do it, too!

These are the things which give meaning to my life. And this is what we in the Solid Group have consistently been doing over the years.

Prawn

One of our exporting companies, AA Export & Import Corporation, has been competing with the best world-class competitors for almost 25 years.

AA EXICO, incidentally, pioneered the pond culturing of black tiger prawns in the Philippines. Before, the prawn business was a hit-and-miss industry; fishermen engaged in deep-sea fishing would sell the prawns they would find entangled in their nets to processors who could freeze these ptawns and sell them abroad. The quantities were never huge, but nonetheless, they fulfilled a ready need.

With pond culturing, AA EXICO was able to stabilize the quantities and quality, of the prawns. What's more, the company has been able to generate employment for around a thousand of our countrymen.

But AA EXICO did more than introduce systems into prawn production.

Having good production techniques and good products is no guarantee that people will buy from you.

Take prawns, for example. As I stated, AA EXICO's main product is black tiger prawn - also known in the vernacular as *"sugpo."*

When we were introducing this product to Japan, we were surprised that the Japanese did not even want to try the product. This was because the Japanese have an aversion to the color black. We had to cook *"sugpo"* in front of the Japanese to show them that the black tiger prawns turn a nice pinkish red when cooked. Only then did the Japanese consent to taste it.

I am glad to report that Japanese consumers have been tasting and buying AA prawns regularly since that time. I am also proud to say that AA EXICO is now the biggest Philippine prawn exporter not only to Japan but also to Canada, Europe, and the United States.

Kita   -

Another one of our exporting companies is Kita Corporation. Kita is engaged in consumer electronic product assembly (on contract basis) for Aiwa Corporation of Japan.

What is remarkable about Kita is that it is the only assembly facility of its size and scope located in Clark Field in Pampanga. We have put in a world-class production facility in a province that has suffered so much in terms of natural calamities.

We have done this despite the fact that we co-own an industrial estate in Laguna - not because we are masochists or fools but because we feel Pampanga needs Kita more.

Kita's production capacity could easily reach one million units a year - more than twice the current Philippine market size of color TV sets. We were able to start up the company late last year - within six months from the time we first thought of putting it up. From that time on, Kita has been steadily producing color TV sets and audio products that Aiwa Corporation has exported to Japan and Europe.

This is certainly a tribute to the extraordinary talents of our engineers. Neither la- har nor dust storms nor locusts nor lack of electricity and ventilation could stop them from doing their jobs and doing them well. I have to say that not only does the Solid Group owe them a lot, but the Philippines does so as well, bringing in much-needed foreign exchange.

We have to remember that both Indonesia and China offer lower wage rates than the Philippines, and that Malaysia and Thailand have more supporting component ' plants that could readily sell to the local market. Despite all these drawbacks, our Kita Corporation has learned not only to survive but to thrive.

But it is not only our exporting companies which are carrying the brunt of the fight against foreign competitors. Our domestic companies have also been doing more than their fair share.

Solid Corporation

Our main company, Solid Corporation, the manufacturing, distribution, and service licensee of Sony Corporation of Japan, has invested in a new electronic products assembly plant in Laguna. This plant is designed with the provisions for high-end consumer electronic products assembly using more sophisticated technology.

Solid Corporation is a unique company, especially when we consider the Sony way of doing business. Solid has remained the only non-Sony owned, non-Sony managed production facility operating within the Sony production world.

This was a feat that took us eight years to accomplish. I had to go personally to Japan to talk to the senior Sony officials to ' let our Filipino engineers have a chance to operate the plant on their own. Sony wisely acceded to this request, and since that time, more than 25 years ago, the Solid electronics plant has not seen a single Japanese engineer get involved in its operations.

Solid's marketing group has also carried its own fair share of the effort to build up the Sony name. Our marketing people have concocted campaigns that localized Sony's global marketing strategies.

Our sales people continue to bring unique Filipino touch to our relations with the dealers. In terms of product management, our marketing people managed to boost the Sony Betamax to market leadership in the Philippines, despite the fact that worldwide, the beta format lost out to the VHS format.

A few years ago, we discontinued the Betamax and launched the Sony View Top VHS models, and Sony rapidly rose to dominant market leadership in this product category.

Our Sony Trinitron color TVs - made in the Philippines by our Solid factories and sold by Filipino employees of our marketing group - are also dominant market leaders, despite the presence of direct subsidiaries of giant Japanese companies.

So you see, the Solid Group is already engaged in competition with exceptionally good, world-class opponents. In fact, we are energized by this competition as it makes us better persons and businessmen.

Stiff wind

Competition is like a strong, stiff wind. It can make you do either of two things: give up and, consequently, get blown away; or, make you resolve to buckle down to work and walk right through the storm.

There is this TV advertisement of a universal bank which is very well done. It shows a huge globe hurtling toward a very frightened businessman, with a booming voiceover asking, "Is your company ready for global competition?" It gives you the impression that if your company is not ready, then world-class competition will roll right over you. But I think the question comes too late. World-class competition is already here.

Are our manufacturing companies, therefore, doomed? In this era of tumbling tariffs, does it still make sense to make things in the Philippines rather than importing them on a completely built up basis? Can we really compete against the giants who have seemingly inexhaustible sources of cash?

I hope my examples about our companies within the Solid Group have shown you that we, as Filipinos, can indeed compete. We have shown this in fields as disparate as agribusiness and electronics. We have shown this in other businesses as well, ranging from domestic and international trade, to plastics, to industrial estate development, and car manufacturing.

For the most part, we made do without the benefit of exhaustive and tiresome research. We have relied mostly on accumulated experience, business sense, and the unerring feel for filling people's needs. Other companies can do no less.

No better time

This is the best of times, this is the worst of times.

For Filipinos who have enough guts and resolve to do battle with foreign competitors, there is no better time to do it than now - for the market is expanding and buyer confidence is high.

But for Filipinos who would rather hide behind the skirts of government and insist on concessions or franchises or unfair advantage, this new era of the open economy is the worst of times.

Also, this is the worst of times for Filipino companies which have solely developed their investments, capabilities in their relation with foreign brand owners, who might think that the new order allows them to gobble up the business in the Philippines.

How you look at the situation depends on your temperament and your courage. I do hope you take heart, get on with your work, and by God, let us push this country forward. Do not rely on government to give us largess. We can do it with our will and limited resources.

We only want two things from government: First, give us a peaceful environment to do our work. Second, give us good governance.

Both are enough, much more than enough.

And from all of us, whatever, wherever, however our work be as academics, professionals, entrepreneurs -- our best contribution to nation-building is for each of us to pay the taxes due to government. Government can't function without funds. We need each other to prosper.

XII Dr. Jose Rizal: Quality of Being is Quality of Living

Commencement Speech before graduates of the University of the East College of Law, College of Dentistry, and Graduate School; April 24, 1996

In 1896, exactly one hundred years ago, someone as full of promise as you, new graduates, gave his life for his people, and country.

He lived in an era of domination, corruption, abuse, poverty, violence and discrimination. Amidst the unjust and cruel society, he fought against the establishment. He spoke openly and wrote actively that the people may know and the world may hear of the plight and aspiration of Filipinos.

Like many of you young graduates, he was a man of letters, the arts and the sciences. He used his knowledge, his intelligence and his skills for the cause of serving his fellowmen by exposing the evils and injustice and demanding integrity and reform. For this cause, he was killed by the establishment.

His name was Jose Rizal. Dr. Jose Rizal called young Filipinos like you the "Hope of the Motherland." He believed that with your idealism, you could right the wrongs of your elders.

To honor him on the centennial of his martyrdom, I was thinking of dedicating this talk to his memory, to his legacy for young Filipinos like you.

Doubts

But I was assailed by doubts.

Of what use is another talk on Rizal? We have become so jaded to countless speeches, countless writings about Rizal. We have talked him to death. Every year, many politicians dust off and recycle past speeches to deliver during his birth and death anniversaries. They try to outdo each other in rhetoric but the words ring false and hollow because we know that after they deliver their speeches, they do the exact opposite of what they just said about Rizal's legacy. Have we failed him? Do we keep him alive in our hearts for his sacrifice and for what he did for our people?

Forgetting Rizal

It is ironic that in immortalizing Rizal, we have forgotten him.

We have reduced him to concrete monuments that serve as street markers. We have literally named streets and movie houses after him.

We have caricatured him into a required school subject.

We read his books not to understand and feel him but to pass our exams. We have trivialized him: *Dinikit pa natin iyong mukha niya saposporo* (We even stuck his face on a box of matches).

We have lost sight of the fact that Dr. Jose Rizal would prefer to live in the hearts and minds of his people than be a lifeless street marker.

Let us be reminded of the ultimate sacrifice he made. No love is greater than to lay down one's life for one's fellowmen. In dying, Jose Rizal left a legacy that the youth whom he called the "Hope of the Motherland" will take up the challenge to continue the struggle against the violence, criminality, corruption, injustice, indecency and poverty of our society.

Integrity

It is a fight that demands integrity from ourselves and from others. This is your cause. As you possess the power of knowledge gained from this institution, the University of the East, the power of experience gained through your association from all who affected your ways of life, you now go into a new world far more complex than the one you've so far lived in.

How will you leave your imprint in this challenging new life? You need not die like Rizal. But in a way, your way of living may even be more demanding than dying. It's easier to die right than to live right. How do we live right?

Quality of Being begets Quality of Living

I submit that one possible way we can do this is by being concerned not just with Quality of Living but, equally if not more importantly, with Quality of Being.

There is nothing wrong with being concerned about Quality of Living as it is commonly understood. Of course, we must make sure that we earn enough to meet our basic needs such as food, shelter, clothing, education, health care, and the like.

But it should not be, it need not be, at the cost of losing our Quality of Being, our soul.

I want to prove that to improve our Quality of Living, we must improve our Quality of Being.

What is Quality of Being?

But first, what exactly is "Quality of Being?" I would define its essence as faith in God, obedience to His will, patriotism, integrity, honesty, hard work, genuine concern for others, real commitment to play by fair and just rules. It is the exact opposite of hypocrisy, corruption, self-centeredness, mindless and heartless profiteering, apathy, opportunism, violence, exploitation and oppression of our fellow beings.

I know that many will say: *"Makakain ba iyang 'Quality of Being' na iyan? Madaling sabihin iyan kung marami ka nang pera. Pero kung namamatay ka na sa gutom, anong 'Quality of Being' na iyan?"* (Can we eat Quality of Being? It's easy to talk of such things when you have lots of money. But when you're dying of hunger, what's Quality of Being?)

Let me prove those who say that wrong — not by citing theories and abstract principles but by giving actual examples from my own life.

Poorer than you

I started out poorer than perhaps many of you here.

I never even experienced putting on a toga and marching to receive my diploma. I earned my degrees in Education, English, and Law through evening classes because I had to work during the day.

I come from the poor province of Leyte. My father passed away when I was only three years old.

My mother was widowed before she was 30 and on her shoulders fell the burden of raising six children.

We eked out a living in Tacloban, Leyte, by making and selling shoes and slippers.

I was not spared from household chores like washing clothes, cleaning the house, fetching water from the market and running all sorts of errands. During the Japanese occupation, I rented out comic books, sold tomatoes in the market and right after the war, I was a waitress in our small restaurant where I served fried chicken and fried noodles to American GIs.

We started our business from rock bottom. We had no economic resources, no political connections.

It was a slow, arduous and painful climb for us in business.

I have to thank my mother for instilling in me the basic values of hard work, fair play and decency. These values were my strength and my tools. I did not shim hard work and manual labor. I developed an inner strength and a gutsy stomach to take falls, disappointments and failures and otherwise cope with hardships. She taught me to be patient and to persevere. I also learned from her the uncanny ability to identify opportunities.

My credo in the worth of work reflects the legacy left me by my mother. To share what I have for the success of others has been a lifelong objective. This trait of sharing belongs to my mother who believed that compassion expressed sincerely to every man, woman, and child bestows a calmer and collected personality to the giver. To me, this is the essence of accomplishment in life.

I hope the examples I have given from my early life provide clear proof that poverty is not reason to compromise "Quality of Being"; that in fact, maintaining Quality of Being can be one's ticket to a higher Quality of Living.

But how does Quality of Being fare in the tough world of business, where compromise is often the name of the game, where refusing to compromise principles can mean losing millions? Let me give you actual examples from my entrepreneurial life.

Solid

Solid Corporation has the distinct honor of being the Exclusive Manufacturer of Sony products in the Philippines while retaining 100% Filipino management and workforce.

Through the years, we have maintained leadership in both our local and export operations.

Solid Corporation is a shining example of a Filipino corporation succeeding in a field dominated by multinationals.

It has continually belied the myth that only multinational companies can succeed in this industry. I am particularly proud of this accomplishment because it proves that I was right in making the Filipino the focus of my vision, in anchoring my strong faith in our country and people.

Black Tiger Prawn

Another example is my experience under AA Export and Import Corporation which pioneered the international marketing of black tiger prawn.

At first, the Japanese did not like the black tiger prawn because of its color. I had to personally go to Japan and demonstrate that the black tiger, when cooked, would turn into a deliciously reddish color. Today, because of Filipino ingenuity, it is accepted not only in Japan but all over the world.

We hardly imagined that it would grow into an industry that would create jobs in the countryside, improve the lives of the fishermen and farmers, and contribute one quarter of a billion U.S. dollars annually to the country's export revenue.

In 1984, when our economy was in shambles and "Jobo Bills" (named after then Central Bank Governor Jose "Jobo" Fernandez) of the Central Bank were peddled at 45% interest, I decided to put up a P20 million prawn processing plant in Bacolod, when nobody had faith in Negros Occidental due to the collapse of the sugar industry.

I patiently waited for two years before any prawns from growers could be processed to serve as start-up production for our plant.   *

Inspired by our vision, the Negrenses rose again and the prawn export industry became the big industry that it is today.

If business were to exist only to earn profits, it would have been far easier to put the P20 million in Jobo Bills and I would have doubled my money in a short time. However, stocks and Jobo Bills pale against my trust in the Filipinos. My plant created hundreds of jobs, earned foreign exchange, increased revenues for both local and national government and upheld the Filipino.

People's Car

The third example is the People's Car experience.

Columbian Autocar Corporation espoused the cause of the People's Car because I felt that Filipinos deserve a less expensive mode of transportation than what was being offered at the time by the three big Japanese-led car manufacturers.

I was rebuffed and discouraged again and again but I kept knocking on doors that were being kept shut by vested interests of the big car assemblers of the time. By sheer persistence on the vision of the people's car, we finally broke down the last barrier and the People's Car category was born.

We introduced the Kia Pride, the first- ever People's Car brand in the market. Until then only three Japanese car brands could be seen on the streets. It took me 18' months to fight this cause before change finally came. Today, owning a vehicle for business or pleasure is no longer a reserve for the rich but a reality for the working Filipino.

Laguna International Industrial Park

Still another example of a change process is our joint-venture industrial estate development company, Laguna International Industrial Park (LIIP).

This 109-hectare industrial estate features facilities investors would look for in a business site: widely paved roads, water supply, telecommunication facilities, even an interchange and public barangay roads worth P80 million which we donated to the Philippine government.

We began development for the LIIP in 1990, at a time when no businessman would seriously think about investing in the Philippines as this was immediately after the December 1989 coup, a coup which closed business in the financial center in Makati and threatened to topple the Cory Aquino government.

We had the full consent of the farmers and the government, but still the process took more than two years of hard work brought about by government bureaucracy - and intervention. But our hearts stayed constant. Despite the political and economic uncertainty, we were steadfast in our belief that the anxiety would soon pass and very soon, there will be a need for first class industrial parks for investors to park their investments in the Philippines.

Kita Corporation

Lastly, I would like to cite the Kita experience.

Kita Corporation, located in the Clark Special Economic Zone, is the company we have set up to manufacture "AIWA" brand color TV for export to Japan.

When we first went to Clark to survey the area, all we saw was an ashfall-covered place with no electricity and water.

The team was ready to pack up and locate our plant to our very own site in Laguna where we had earmarked hectares for this project. It has its advantages.

The site was beautifully located in Laguna. Electric power and telephone lines are already available. Widely paved and cemented roads with trees blooming fill the air. It's fronting the same extension of EDSA and only about 20 kilometers to the Manila Port.

With lots of talented workforce too. Why did I ever have to search far?

But I stopped for a moment and looked at the potentials beyond the desolation.

It was then I was able to put together a vision that would overcome the natural obstacles and tap a local workforce that was highly trainable and very motivated, itching for a chance to show what it could do.

I believe that it is the Lord's will that people do things sometimes out of the context of common sense. There is a purpose and plan designed by the Lord. We have to pause and listen to His voice.

Japanese Opposition

At the start, my Japanese partners were very much against the idea of setting up Kita Corporation in Clark. They wanted to establish the factory in a place like Laguna to avoid all the problems present in Clark, plus the convenience of being near the urban comforts of Metro Manila.

They must have thought I had taken leave of my senses to be so stubborn on building the plant in Clark Field. After a series of meetings, finally, they gave up trying to convince me

Nightmarish

Our first few months in building the factory in Clark were nightmarish. Against all odds, we persisted against the elements. We trucked in water and rolled in our own generator during the construction. We bussed in our workers to make sure they got in on time. We struggled with bureaucracy and narrow-minded individuals every step of the way. We persisted in our vision and found others who shared and supported our decision and worked with us just as hard.

Today, our persistence has borne fruit and continues to bear even more. The vision becomes clearer to more people and integrity and excellence have become our standard way of life. I pursued the "Quality of Being" while I persevered in my vision—the Vision of Doin the Unthinkable and Making it Work for the Common Good.

Business with Values

I hope the examples I have cited from my business life give solid proof that Quality of Being is not contradictory to entrepreneurial success. My climb in business has been a fulfilling one as this was based on basic moral values, Spartan work ethic, passion to fight for one's belief, care not to injure anyone, and with the consciousness that everything I do must redound to some good for others.

Hope of the Motherland

As you graduate from this great institution of learning and enter the real world to fulfill your destiny as lawyers, dentists, holders of master's and doctorate degrees, I ask you to work shoulder to shoulder to overcome present difficulties and work as one living vital force with a single vision and one heart in order to attain peace and prosperity for the Filipinos.

You must be committed to the proposition that service in its pure state is the paramount order of the day. You must be shining examples of Filipinos with integrity, competence and selfless industry. You must, therefore, put service above self and pursue one single direction to promote the common good of Filipinos.

If you truly love your country, you must render quality and caring service to your country and people.

Quality service has no relation whatsoever to the loftiness of one's position. I define quality service as work which is done sincerely, honestly and competently by persons who are striving for the common good — who are not overwhelmed by thoughts of mere selfish gain or personal glory.

Let each of us then who has a role in nation-building contribute in his own way, but let us never forget that the common good is far greater than personal or material gain.

Core Values

Amidst temptations, let us stand by these good values. Let us not be tempted to take the path to glory and wealth through illegal shortcuts, self-gain compromises, and collusion with corrupt persons.

Some of the core values we must uphold are:

* Resist the dole-out mentality.
* Stand on your own merits.
* Play by the rules.

Do not seek concessions which only you can enjoy. You can see how the behest loans and monopolies have benefited a few but ruined our economy.

We should be more aggressive in voicing truth and justice. As Longfellow said: "Be not like dumb driven cattle. Be a hero in the strife."

Do not become drunk with the power of office, if ever you are appointed to high government or private sector posts. Avoid the hypocrisy of mouthing promises without meaning them.

Avoid fault-finding. Instead of just uttering criticism for the sake of criticizing, suggest improvements.

Have pride in your work, no matter how menial it may be.

In life, it is ultimately the person who has the most positive attitude who will succeed.

Success comes to those who love work and honor God.

No matter what you may be, just strive to become the best. The best includes the Quality of Being!

I started my talk with the question - How do we live right? By pursuing a life with a Quality of Being.

Abou Ben Adhem

Before I end, let me remind you of Abou Ben Adhem, who lived in his time and woke one night to see an angel writing in a book. Abou Ben Adhem asked "What writest thou?' and the angel replied: "The names of those who profess to love the Lord."

"And is mine one?" said Abou. "Nay, not so," replied the angel.

So Abou said: "Write me then as one who loves his fellowmen."

The angel left. The next night, the angel came and showed him the names of those whom God loves best. And lo! Adhem's name led all the rest!

Dear graduates, I pray that we will all be like Abou Ben Adhem.

I pray that we will all be filled with a genuine desire to love and serve our fellowmen.

This is the challenge to you, young graduates, as you embark on your journey to the new chapter in your lives.

Live by this edict and glorify God with your good deeds.

Do not falter. You owe it to your parents. You owe it to a great Filipino named Jose Rizal who gave his life one-hundred years ago to give you a better future. You owe it to your country and people. You owe it to yourself.

Build a nation with great values so your children will inherit a legacy greater than what we, your elders, have left you.

XIII Strategic Partnerships for Globalization

Mid-year Business Forum of the Corporate Planning Society of the Philippines and PICPA; The Manila Peninsula Hotel, June 27, 1996

The idea of forming strategic partnerships for globalization is not difficult to comprehend.

Among corporate planners and business professionals the concept of synergy is nothing new. Our own *bayanihan* spirit almost assures understanding of what a partnership is all about.

A partnership could mean anything from a simple alliance, a brotherhood, a fellowship, or a union, at least between two parties. Describing one as a "strategic partnership," especially in the context of globalization, evokes visions of grandiose alliance, a unity of purpose, and cross- cultural or transnational boundaries.

Main interest: Self-interest

The participants in global strategic partnerships include governments, big business, and special interest groups. Almost always, the reasons behind such partnerships go beyond pure altruism. The desire to further one's own ends often supersedes all other reasons.

Here then starts the difference between a partnership and a relationship based on exploitation.

Real partners show and practice mutual respect and admiration for each other's capability, competence, and integrity.

Partners also believe in "win-win" relationships and further realize the inevitability of having one's future prospects intertwined with those of the other. Goal congruence is often not difficult to achieve in the ideal partnership.

Capability, Competence, Integrity

Let me then focus on the three attributes I earlier pointer out:

capability, competence, and integrity. There are countless others you may be able to think of, but let me just dwell on these three. I will attempt to explain in my own humble way what I think these are and why I think they are critical.

First, capability. "Capability" is the catch-all phrase I use to represent the totality of resources a prospective partner intends to bring into the partnership to help deliver the most effective and efficient services, or produce the total quality product.

One hitches his fortunes with another because of the firm belief that the other's resources would be a perfect complement to existing capabilities. Logically, if one has nothing to show in terms of capability, no partner is forthcoming.

Role of Government

At this point, I cannot help but mention government in this discussion, with some apologies of course, to our respected members of the cabinet here present.

If strategic partnership for globalization is the staple, the role government plays cannot be dismissed. It is no exaggeration, in fact, that any discussion of capability must necessarily include what government is and is not doing.

Prospective partners look at opportunities, threats, stability, convenience, and efficiencies. These can only be assured if the required infrastructures are in place, government policies are precise and consistent, the bureaucracy is lean and civil servants are honest, dedicated, and true.

I speak of these not out of desire to pick on our leaders and policy makers, but as one with experiences, both pleasant and sad, in contending with that mammoth of an organization called government.

I wrote in the past about how we almost abandoned a major project, if not for the timely intervention of a few dedicated and responsible professionals in government who saw the light in what we were doing and waived the endless list of senseless bureaucratic requirements. Do we have more, or less, of these people now in government?

Infrastructure

Let's talk infrastructure too.

Our company is involved in some manufacturing activities in the former Clark Air Force Base. We established this facility consistent with our belief and faith in the resiliency of the Filipino spirit, and with the modest aim of contributing to economic development.

We have partners in this enterprise, partners who share with us our dreams and vision and who believe that we are a strategic, integral part of their overall corporate objectives, just as we also view them in the same light.

In the development of this enterprise and in nurturing this partnership, there were times we had to be apologetic to our partners because there appeared serious doubts about our capability.

When there's no road where there is supposed to be one, when lights don't light, when a telephone line is but a dream, how do you explain these to your partner?

We are also aware of Philippines 2000 and everything it is supposed to stand for.

In the pursuit of that exalted status of an industrialized country, there always exists the temptation to rush development and deploy resources less than efficiently.

Liberalization

In a bid to attract investors (and prospective partners), liberalization is the oft-repeated solution bruited about which is supposed to bring down protectionism, encourage efficiencies, and penalize the weak.

This scenario assumes that the major players have almost equal capabilities and that innovation, imagination, daring, persistence, decisiveness, and public relations will spell the difference.

Let's assume that we have all these and more, are we really capable in terms of structures, policies, business and political climate to stand up to the big guys, stare them down, and say, we are equally worth to be a partner?

Unless we earn respectability in terms of capability, no partnership could ensue. Instead exploitation will remain the order of the day. How many companies will reel under the pressure of uneven competition and eventually fold up?

There will be survivors of course. The semiconductor companies will still be there, as well as others not too dependent on local efficiencies.

For sure we will appreciate the value added to their imports which are eventually re-exported after processing.

But real strategic partnership does not mean merely providing a convenient halfway house between manufacturing operations.

It involves offering one's total capabilities to complement another's for the purpose of creating something of further value, the generation of wealth, and improvement of the quality of life.

Competence

Competence assures proficiency, efficiency and effectiveness in the utilization of one's avowed capabilities.

The collective competence of a nation is the sum of total skills in, knowledge of, and training and preparation for, the various tasks of nation building and national development. Such competencies have to be relevant and must be used as originally intended. It is a monumental waste of resources to train people to become teachers, nurses, and other specific disciplines, only to deploy them as domestic helpers abroad.

It is also difficult to talk of competence without touching on the educational system. After all, formal education is still the single most important bastion of knowledge and skills. Almost every school has in its mission, vision, and goals something about globalization and the need to produce graduates who meet international standards.

What really is the profile of this graduate? Almost surely, he must have good analytical skills, is an excellent communicator, is aware of cultural differences, has an international perspective, and is familiar with information technology. Are school curricula, as now designed and implemented, global in orientation? How has teaching strategies changed in the last decade or sq to meet the new challenges?

Integrity

And finally integrity. A few months back I spoke before distinguished members of the Rotary Club of Manila and I remember distinctly exclaiming that we must demand integrity in all our dealings.

There can be no compromise as far as integrity is concerned.

In our company, and I'm sure in many others, it is demanded at all levels of the corporate organization, in all dealings, in all work and personal relations. Integrity must pervade all aspects of corporate, social and personal cultures.

When we try to reach out beyond our borders, talk to total strangers and convince them to become strategic, long-term partners, what could be better than to start in an atmosphere of mutual trust and confidence.

Integrity is not just for close encounters of the initial kind. It must be there always and forever, otherwise no partnership will endure. I know. I've seen it work.

In my experience, this often meant simply being aware what one's role in nation building is.

All it takes is integrity

Nobody is lowly enough as to be dismissed as having an

insignificant role in the formidable task of nation building. Each one has a role, and living that role as God meant it to be, is often all it takes for integrity to flourish and become infectious. By this simple test, it is easy to see whether integrity is in and around somebody.

Strategic partners could be as warm and as spontaneous as the simplest handshake. That these are being pursued in the desire to expand global horizons should not necessarily make them complicated.

The basics remain the same. Be capable; be competent, and have integrity. A partner with integrity, fairness and trustworthiness may be just around the comer.

XIV
The Entrepreneur's Role in Countryside Development

22nd Annual Conference of the Financial Executives Institute of the Philippines; Holiday Inn Resort, Clark Field, Pampanga; October 18,1996

Ladies and gentlemen, allow me at the outset to thank you for the invitation to speak to you today.

When I first received the invitation and saw the topic I was requested to speak about, my initial knee-jerk reaction was to ask, "Who wants to know?" I thought all along that other than the ever-present civil servant, there is nobody else in the countryside but the entrepreneur. There are no managers in the countryside; is there anybody from FINEX?

Almost embarrassing

The countryside I have in mind is like the CALABARZON area, but the countryside of the subsistence farmer and fisherman where the vast majority of our countrymen live, and where in some places time has virtually stood still. Anybody in the countryside who spurs economic activity by providing a service or adding value to a product through further processing should fit our definition of the entrepreneur. It is almost embarrassing to define the role of the entrepreneur in countryside development.

Indeed who among us does not really know what that role is?

If we consider that we are not at the cutting edge of technological development, and considering the massive investments required to put up industries, it is obvious that not all the industrialists combined could rescue the countryside from neglect. If there is anybody who could keep the countryside going, it is the entrepreneur. You find him in every trader, producer, processor, or service provider engaged in micro or small enterprises.

They truly add value to their own little economies and generate at least one additional job. Every single job they generate means one less squatter family for Metro Manila or some other metropolis. Yet there seems to be no end to the multitude coming to the city from the countryside. We are all witness to the congestion in the cities.

Squatter colonies are sprouting all over, increasing the strain on the city's resources and capability to provide basic services like health and education.

The squalor and subhuman conditions in the city's blighted areas cannot compare with the freshness, vigor, serenity, and peace in the countryside. But still they come to the city because, as they say, there is nothing in the countryside; nothing in terms of a steady income, nothing in terms of opportunities.

Simply neglected?

Is the countryside so bereft of entrepreneurs and innovators, or has it simply been neglected, deprived of resources and skills necessary for successful enterprise development.

I am afraid the latter is the case. We have all heard of Imperial Manila, that sarcastic allusion to the government's predilection to[1] control the life and times of the nation from national offices and headquarters based in Manila.

Unfortunately, such sorry state is not limited to government service. The private sector could also be equally guilty of this tendency to concentrate resources and decision-making in the cities.

Elusive capital

Of all the resources that countryside entrepreneurs need, nothing comes readily to mind than capital and financing. There is no better place and time than here and now to discuss capital and financing for the entrepreneur, for the simple reason that we have here today an assembly of the best and influential minds in the field of finance.

Many business failures and missed opportunities are direct results of inadequate capital or financing.

I've seen friends and acquaintances, some with the most brilliant and innovative ideas, lose their businesses either because of inadequate or ill-timed financing.

Yet these businesses were not even in the countryside, but in the metropolis where there is access to communications, and coffee with the bank manager is as regular as can be. How much more difficult could it be for the countryside entrepreneur whose only access to capital and credit is your friendly loan shark.

To be sure, there have been a lot of innovations in the delivery of financial services; but all the financial re-engineering are happening in the big-time world of corporate and international finance. Surely there had been and there still are financing packages ostensibly for small and medium industries. However, I have some problems with the definition of SMEs. By my standards, and probably of many others, a 10 to 50 million pesos business is not small.

Not too many can borrow that much on sheer project viability. Even at 10% equity, very few will have a million to start.

I also believe that most businesses with the potential to become a small enterprise do not necessarily need a million to start. With proper management, fast turnover, and adequate controls, these businesses just might succeed with a few hundred thousand pesos to start.

Not rich or poor enough

While this group may have the brightest potential to become multi-million businesses, I feel this is where the greatest business failures are.

Those in this category are a miserable lot. They are not rich; nor do they have enough properties to raise the amount needed. Their needs are too big for microlending, yet too small and unattractive to banks.

We find in this group those who are trying to supplement a regular salary (the business not big enough yet to warrant resignation or retirement), one who just lost a job or is unemployable, who has no rich relatives, and has little or no collateral. In the countryside, almost all are natives of the place who have no plans of migrating or moving elsewhere.

The commercial banks have not been of much help. It is a no-man's land as far as they are concerned despite claims to the contrary.

While most of them claim to be conduits for SME funds, they do not have the interest, nor the attitude, nor the training to help out this sector. The same goes for so- called development banks.

I cannot blame these financial institutions for their business sense. It is virtually risk-free and more profitable to lend out to somebody who does not need the money.

Who would be interested therefore in start-up businesses, where the future is uncertain, and the collateral is nil.

There is therefore this big divide that start-up businesses have to cross before they can succeed. If they survive the loan sharks along the way, they are lucky.

This sector is also often denied access to sound management advice.

At the start-up stage, setting up the proper controls also often is a low-priority concern. Obviously, these businesses cannot afford expensive professional services and the cost of establishing the necessary controls could be prohibitive.

Immense trials of entrepreneurs

I see opportunities in the areas mentioned above which may require innovations in the way financial and management advisory services could be delivered to start-up businesses.

I feel, for example, that as much as the entrepreneur himself, the prospective financier (whether venture capitalist or banker) must also have the entrepreneurial spirit.

Entrepreneurs think and act differently in many ways that may not be understood by your ordinary bank manager or analyst.

Nothing comes close to the anxieties and tensions of the entrepreneur. Meeting the next payroll, paying suppliers, bank loans maturing, checks bouncing, delivery schedules to meet, quality control, employee unrest, inadequate insurance, government bureaucracy, and so many other daily and strategic concerns all combine for a nerve-wracking experience that most people can never imagine.

I, for example, suffered through three miscarriages which I attribute to entrepreneurial stress. If I succeeded, it is through my perseverance and refusal to quit.

But I say to all of you, please help the poor entrepreneur. I hope you could extend to him the same courtesies you could give your valued clients. If you must have coffee with your biggest depositor, I hope you will not have the insensitivity to let the entrepreneur wait two hours for his turn. He might be missing an opportunity already.

New concept needed

The structure, terms, form and content of financing arrangements may also need a whole new concept. There is need to review and rethink approaches to credit evaluation, the tools for analysis, and information gathering and validation. Emphasis may, for example, be given to potential risk analysis, personal background investigation, and behavior prediction. Credit analysts should be re-oriented and trained in these new tools and approaches.

Management services and operations review should also become as much tools for the financier as they are for the entrepreneur, the former to better protect his exposure; the latter to ensure success and growth for the enterprise. All these will have to be done the most efficient and reliable way, at the least cost affordable to the entrepreneur while at the same time guaranteeing the safety of, and a return on, the investment of the service provider.

Micro-lending ordeal

It must be stressed that entrepreneurship will not be served through microlending. Jesus said that there will be poor always that, by divine design, most of the beneficiaries of micro-lending are destined to stay poor, unless there is a way to graduate to the ranks of small enterprises. Poverty alleviation is a sentimental, politically correct endeavor. But the concern is merely to make life a little better.

Venture capital is also one potential area where little progress has been made.

There is a need to rethink the approaches towards venture capital. It cannot be implemented under the same rules of ordinary lending and with the attitude of a creditor.

There must be a long-term commitment of funds and a willingness to share management responsibilities and business risk. Collateral should not be an issue. Instead, project viability, sound business fundamentals, and management competence and integrity should be given premium above all the others.

The venture capitalist must also provide attractive options to the entrepreneur to guarantee the latter's continued interest in the enterprise.

Distortion of SME law

There is a law intended to provide some credit for SMEs. This is Republic Act 9501, the Magna Carta for Micro, Small, and Medium Enterprises.

However, most banks interpret compliance with this law by simply shifting the 10% allotment for foreign currency deposits, thus releasing them from their obligation to give 10% to the SMEs. They find the latter cumbersome, riddled by unknowns, and ever risky.

This circumvents the letter and spirit of the law but it is a practice that deprives many SMEs from access to much-needed funds for working capital.

I hope I have succeeded in sharing with you today some of my thoughts. Nothing arouses my passion more than the trials and tribulations of the entrepreneur.

I congratulate your group for remembering the countryside

entrepreneur. I pray that this conference will lead to positive development towards improving their plight.

Thank you very much and have a good day.

XV
Is It Good for the Filipino?

Acceptance of TOP WOMAN BUSINESS OWNER IN THE COUNTRY TODAY Award given during the WOMEN IN BUSINESS CONFERENCE '96; Dusit Hotel Nikko, Makati; November 21, 1996

Ladies and gentlemen, good afternoon.

The award you have bestowed on me as the "Top Woman Business Owner in the Country Today" feels too large for a small woman like me. I am less than five feet tall and, as I often teased my late mother, I must have stopped growing because of the heavy pails of water on my shoulders when I was a child in Leyte.

During those hard, poverty-stricken days, it was never in my wildest dreams that one day I would stand in this beautiful ballroom before such distinguished women and men as you, receiving award such as this.

The road from Leyte to this moment has been long and difficult beyond words. I therefore have no words to express the meaning of this award. I can only thank you.

This award is doubly significant for me because it comes from the gender some consider superior: my fellow women, gathered here in this WOMEN IN BUSINESS CONFERENCE '96. I noticed, though, that the invitation was signed by a man named Rafael A. Francisco. I just hope he has earned the distinction of being an honorary woman.

You have asked me to talk about my insights and experiences as a woman business executive. If like the Arabs of old we had a thousand and one nights, perhaps I could begin to tell you about what I've learned from the time I was a child-entrepreneur selling tomatoes in the, streets of Leyte and renting out comic books.

For now, let me focus on one message.

Bottom line

To my mind, the bottom <u>line</u> about any undertaking is the question: Is it good for the Filipino?

Entrepreneurship is synonymous to tremendous risk, great sacrifice, and greater work. But if a business project will do good to the greatest number of Filipinos, then it is worth all the risk, sacrifice, and hard work. Conversely, if something is bad for the Filipino, be it in business, politics, or culture, then it is incumbent on every Filipino to have the courage to speak and act against it.

We have the great challenge of living in the most frenetic period in the history of human race. The pace of change in the past few decades has been a million times faster than all the past centuries combined. As we enter the 21st century, that pace can only become faster, with technology growing by leaps and bounds every second worldwide, such that a new product seems to become obsolete shortly after it is launched.

Supreme irony

At this very moment, our nation is hosting APEC, a gathering of 18 world leaders with their respective contingents determined to push regional cooperation, bringing free trade to new heights of freedom by dismantling all protectionist barriers. This will most likely favor the developed countries over poor nations like the Philippines.

The supreme irony here is that the staunchest advocates of free trade would not have attained their present strength if they had not been highly efficient and effective protectionists in the past.

In a level playing field, free trade would be beautiful and would unleash our best potentials. But in a highly lopsided situation, the implications are obviously ominous, portentous of grave danger.

Have the most avid supporters of APEC with its fast-track liberalization policies and programs also studied the matter thoroughly?

Have they thoroughly studied the implications on the poor and weak sectors?

Have they truly provided adequate safety nets? Where are they? What are they? How will the transition be effected to ensure that liberalization will redound to the Filipino good?

Listen also to the weak

We should listen to all voices in our society, especially the voice of the weak.

What I understand is if APEC regional cooperation will indeed create the right conditions for shared growth and shared prosperity, then we should work for it, with it, in it, with all our heart and soul. We must be clear, though, on how shared growth and shared prosperity will be translated into our daily lives.

But if we ask ourselves the bottom line question - "Is it good for the Filipino?" - and find that the answer is "Not sure' or "Not clear," not necessarily "No," then we must proceed with caution and study all the detailed implications.

In such a confusing and fast-paced period like our present and unforeseeable future, it is imperative that we do lose sight of our North Star, that we keep ourselves moving in the right direction by asking ourselves the right questions, such as "Is it good for the Filipino?"

Only then will we understand why quality of being is even more important than quality of living.

Only then will we understand why is it correct for Filipino women to have the same opportunity as Filipino men to handle both the board table and the dining table.

Only then will we understand why in the global community of nations, we must not forget our own nation, our own people.

Is it good for the Filipino?

As we sit here this afternoon, as we Filipinos host the most important international summit in Philippine history, let us not forget this question.

Again, my gratitude for the honor you have given me this afternoon. I am very happy and honored to be part of this WOMEN IN BUSINESS CONFERENCE because this is a clear step forward for us Filipino women in our quest for true partnership with our equal - not better - half: our beloved Filipino men.

Hopefully, without being presumptuous, I can say that what's good for Filipino women will also be good for the Filipino people, including the men.

Thank you.

XVI We Must Be Larger than Ourselves

23rd National Capital Region (NCR) Regional Conference of the Philippine
Dental Association; Ramada Hotel, Manila; November 24,1996
There is a poem that goes:

For want of a nail a shoe was lost.
For want of a shoe, a horse was lost.
For want of a horse, a leader was lost.
For want of a leader, a battle was lost.
For want of a battle a kingdom was lost... and all because of a
horseshoe nail.

In much the same way, for want of a good dentist, a very large business deal or literally a kingdom could be lost.

Few tortures can compare with the pain that a rotting tooth gives, and you simply can't work, you can't think, you can't negotiate any deal, you can't win any war when your tooth decides to give you the most excruciating pain imaginable.

And that is why dentists are so important. In a pain-filled world, you are healers of pain.

Larger Pain

But today, I Would like to pose a challenge . . . While the relief and cure you give your patients already constitute a substantial public service, you need not stop there. While it is praiseworthy to work hard to earn more for yourself and your loved ones, you need not stop there.

One hundred years ago, a fellow doctor of yours who was very talented and very handsome, could also have chosen to just have a lucrative practice and go about being an international playboy.

But he saw to the very core of what it means to be a doctor, that the essence of being a doctor is reverence for life, caring profoundly for life, caring profoundly for your fellow human-beings, your fellow-Filipinos, your motherland.

And so, despite all the temptations of living a self-centered bohemian life, Dr. Jose Rizal decided to address not only the individual ills of his patients but also the larger ills of Philippine society. He saw clearly that physical cancer has much in common with social cancer.

As you hold your 23rd NCR Regional Conference, with your timely and beautiful theme of "Unity Towards Service and Professionalism," my challenge to you then is to become larger than yourselves. My challenge to you is to ask you not only "Is it good for me?" but to be large and great enough to ask the bottom line question: "Is it good for the Filipino?"

Cooperation or Destruction?

The need for all of us Filipinos to become larger than ourselves has never been more urgent. At this very moment, our nation is hosting the Asia-Pacific Economic Cooperation or APEC Summit, a gathering of 18 world leaders with their respective contingents determined to push regional cooperation, bringing free trade to new heights of freedom by dismantling all protectionist barriers.

The basic timetable agreed upon for full lifting of protectionist trade barriers is year 2010 for developed countries like the United States and Japan, and year 2020 for developing countries like the Philippines.

In effect, poor and backward nations are given only a 10-year "grace period" to attain the same level of market openness and competitiveness as rich and advanced nations.

Considering the tremendous lead currently enjoyed by advanced nations in terms of financial and technological resources, there is nothing gracious about this "grace period" at all. It appears to be but a token of gesture of consideration.

The situation is made worse by the current administration's overly ambitious plan to fully open up the Philippine economy by year 2003. To meet the 2020 deadline would already be miraculous. To think that we can make it by 2003 verges on being "mentally unable," to use a politically correct and polite term.

The supreme irony here is that the staunchest advocates of free trade would not have attained their present strength if they had not been highly efficient and effective protectionists in the past, as contrasted to our limp, wimpy, unfocused, and generally poor protectionist policies and programs that didn't work.

Really, it's like present heavyweight champion Evander Holyfield challenging a malnourished, light-as-a-feather, poorly trained boxer from Tawi-Tawi to a championship match in Las Vegas. If Holyfield would pick on someone of equal weight, nutrition, and training, it would be a great fight. Otherwise, it will only be pathetic and tragic.

Similarly, in a level playing field, free trade would be beautiful and would unleash our best potentials. But in a highly lopsided situation, the implications are obviously ominous, portentous of grave danger.

Cardinal Sin

It is not much different from the Laurel- Langley Agreement in the early days of our nation's independence when Filipinos and Americans were theoretically given equal rights to do business and own property in each other's country.

The catch was no Filipino could afford to do business in the US.

As a result, only American businessmen benefited from the Agreement since they had all the resources needed to exploit the Philippines.

Cardinal Sin (Archbishop of Manila) has said that the principal goal of APEC is profit for the strong nations.

For such a statement, he has been criticized by the proponents of APEC as not having studied the matter thoroughly and of being narrow-minded.

If it be so, I must ask: Have the most avid supporters of APEC with its fast- track liberalization policies and programs also studied the matter thoroughly? Have they considered all the key details beyond the easy rhetoric, considering that there's much truth in the saying that the devil lies in the details?

For example the matter of "protection of intellectual property rights" under which multinational companies with their sophisticated legal and financial resources, can easily patent even indigenous technologies, so that even herbal medicines like *"pito-pito"* and *"lagundi,"* long-used by generations of poor Filipinos as cheaper alternative medicine will suddenly become branded and unaffordable.

While it is correct to protect intellectual property just like physical property, how do we prevent abuse of its provisions by powerful interests who will take advantage of the ignorance of backward peoples?

Furthermore, have the APEC proponents thoroughly studied the implications on the poor and weak sectors?

Have they truly provided adequate safety nets? Where are they? What are they? How will the transition be effected to ensure that liberalization will redound to the Filipino good?

We should listen to all voices in our society, especially the voice of the weak.

Is it good for the Filipino?

What I understand is if the APEC regional cooperation will indeed create the *right conditions for shared growth and shared prosperity,* then we should work for it, with it, in it, with all our heart and soul.

We must be clear, though, on how shared growth and shared prosperity will be translated into our daily lives.

But if we ask ourselves the bottom line question - "Is it good for the Filipino?" - and find that the answer is "Not sure" or "Not clear," not necessarily "No," then we must proceed with caution and study all the detailed implications.

RP- WTO agreement (1994)

Only two years ago, our President, Fidel V. Ramos, signed our adherence to WTO, subjecting us to their rules and regulations.

Many critics had varying opinions on this act.

Some say that he has hastily signed to something not well studied and well informed to the public, thus bringing us to more difficulties.

Some say that he did this out of his great belief that it's about time we learn to work globally, competitively, and Filipinos can do it, is his slogan.

Some say that he did it out of his *"kayabangan"* (boastfulness). We will always have varying critics.

But I say, let us not be diverted in our concern for our people's welfare.

We must be vigilant. We must be aware of the consequences of what is in store for us and must voice out continuing wrongdoings, good deeds, and bad governance.

We must all understand the implications of globalization, liberalization, and deregulation and not forget our own national interests.

Our work must be for the good of Filipinos and our country.

Be healers of nation

Look up to Dr. Jose Rizal. Why you should get involved in nation-building in your pursuit of your dental career advancement.

Let not your interest be solely focused on your dental activities, a very, noble career, indeed. Look beyond your career and let your voice be heard as well on your aspiration for our national good.

Dr. Jose Rizal was a serious physician. He traveled in Europe to perfect his craft and healed many patients. But his heart went far beyond the healing of patients.

He gave up his career, his life, to heal our country under the yoke and tyranny of Spanish rule.

When asked to cooperate with Imperial Spain and recant his writings, he faced death by musketry in Luneta.

He dreamed and visualized a great Filipino nation where people can sacrifice for the ideals of their country.

He showed us his steadfastness on Filipino integrity. He exposed exploitation, corruption, and the evils of the rulers. He cried, over a hundred years ago, for the cause of the Filipino integrity and his right of choosing death over cooperation with the wrongs of his oppressors for a pittance reward of worldly pleasures.

He is indeed a great Filipino hero, the greatest, our national hero.

Let us emulate his love of country, which was larger than his life. We will not die like Jose Rizal. But we need to live and be larger than ourselves, large enough to ask the question: "Is it good for the Filipino?"

We are all challenged to be true healers of a nation in great pain, to be larger than ourselves.

Thank you.

XVII The Challenge of Making Trade Harmonious and Fair

Talk before the Philippine-Korean
Economic Council (PHILKOREC);
Manila; November 25, 1996

Dr. Rebecco Panlilio, Chairman of the Philippines-Korea Economic Council, Inc. or PHILKOREC, Mr. Lee Son-Young, Chairman of the Korea-Philippines Economic Council or KORPHILEC, Mr. Park Jae-Yoon, Minister of Trade, Industry and Energy, Republic of Korea, Dr. Thomas Aquino, Governor, Board of Investments, Dr. <u>Kim</u> Ki-Whan, Chairman of KOTRA, members of PHILIKOREC and KORPHILEC, ladies and gentlemen. Good morning.

You have asked me to share with you " success stories, from my'personal experiences, regarding Filipino-Korean business partnership.

Let me note, though, that the most impressive success story is the success story of the South Korean people themselves.

Incredible growth

Despite great problems such as seemingly endless tensions with North Korea coupled with domestic unrest, South Korea's real GNP has grown from US$2.3 billion in 1962, when it launched its First Five-Year Economic Development Plan, to US$451.7 billion in 1995. Per capita GNP increased from US$87 in 1962 to US$10,076 in 1995 at current price levels.

This incredible economic growth has been matched by an equally incredible growth in political maturity.

The entire world has watched in awe and admiration the decisive and courageous moves of South Korean President Kim Young Sam, since the inauguration of his administration in February 1993.

The current leadership has demonstrated the courage and political will to convict no less than two past presidents for corruption, abuse of power, and other illegal acts.

One has been sentenced to life imprisonment, the other to death. Both cases are on appeal but in the meantime, both are behind bars.

Real name system

On August 12, 1993, President Kim Young San took a decisive step toward revitalizing the economy and eliminating corruption by announcing the implementation of the long-anticipated real name financial transaction system.

In the past, it had been possible to open accounts and conduct business transactions under false names, directly and indirectly fostering institutionalized corruption and illegal financial dealings.

Deeming this reform as the most important in the creation Of a new Korea, the President announced this action in a Presidential Emergency Decree, stating that the real name system is essential for cutting the dark link between politics and business.

Philippine dummy system

South Korea's real name system is truly a brilliant policy.

One can only wish we had the same system in the Philippines. Its absence is one of the dark aspects of Philippine society.

The mandate in the Philippine constitution to uphold the Filipino in all walks of life has been made inutile in the failure of implementing the right policies.

Many businesses in the Philippines are working under "dummies" that allow foreigners to dominate many sectors of business. Usually, foreigners use Filipino "representatives" (dummies) to enter the retail business. Many Filipinos also use dummies to engage in smuggling and tax evasion.

I pray for our nation's deliverance from this scourge.

Inspiration

President Kim Young San's concrete actions, among many other reforms, are a tremendous source of inspiration especially for other Asian nations aspiring for a political and economic order of similar dynamism, courage, integrity, and maturity.

It is therefore a source of great pride for me to have worked with companies such as Kia of Korea for our people's car project, and with Samsung Co., Ltd., of Korea, for our industrial estate project.

Crusade: People's Car

The people's car project was one of the most difficult and challenging crusades, because it involved breaking the solid Japanese car cartel in the Philippine automotive industry.

Under the administration of President Corazon C. Aquino established through the 1986 "People Power" EDSA Revolt, the car industry was limited to three Japanese car-makers. This limitation was due to a mysterious conviction by government decision-makers that three was the maximum viable number for a healthy Philippine car industry.

In a seller's market situation, the three Japanese car companies deemed it convenient and profitable to focus on car categories affordable only to upper income class Filipinos.

Thus, despite the fact that especially in the urban setting, a vehicle is no longer a luxury but a necessity, the average middle-class Filipinos were denied access to an affordable vehicle which they could use for work and daily family trips.

I saw the great injustice in the prevailing system and decided to do something about it. Thus, I and my business partners looked for a people's car and found it in the Kia Pride, a car produced by Kia of Korea, which combined high quality performance and features with affordability.

But finding the people's car was the easy part. The hard part was getting government approval to market the Kia Pride in the face of determined lobbying by the Japanese car cartel.

Getting the people's car on the road was truly a nerve-wracking experience full of drama, heartaches, and obstacles that we hurdled only through single-minded determination and very hard work. Through it all, Kia of Korea was a solid and reliable partner, sharing both joys and tribulations.

And now, Kia Pride occupies a permanent place of honor in Philippine history as the very first people's car that broke the Japanese car cartel and enabled the ordinary hardworking Filipino to have the car he so rightly deserves to have.

Kia Pride also paved the way for the liberalization of the Philippine car industry, such that now there are numerous car makers, including several more from Korea like Daewoo and Hyundai.

Maybe now there are too many but too many is better than too few because the latter breeds monopolistic franchises and prevents fair competition and free and wide choice for consumers.

It also gave a very clear lesson on the importance of "right timing."

Timing is everything

In my 40 years experience in business, I have discovered that in many instances, the success or failure of a business lies in the timing.

Timing is very important. If we were to fight the Japanese cartel now after giving them additional lead time of 10 years, chances are they would be too strong for us to break. It would be too late or too difficult for latecomers to catch up.

On the other hand, the historical significance of Laguna International Industrial Park or LIIP, our industrial estate joint venture project with Samsung Co., Ltd., of Korea, lies in the fact that it came at one of the darkest periods of our nation's life.

As we may recall, the early nineties were marked by a succession of coup attempts against the Aquino administration which understandably scared off both domestic and foreign investors from the Philippines;

Clearly, what the country needed most then was a solid gesture of faith from the business community to restore investor confidence. Unfortunately, there were few takers because most felt it safer to take a wait-and-see attitude.

I decided to do my bit for my country. Because for me, the bottom line always is the question: Is it good for the Filipino? If the answer is yes, then I willingly meet any risk and do every work required.

Leap of faith

And so, with Samsung, we decided to take a great leap of faith and poured in hundreds of millions of pesos in the development of LIIP, which marked the first industrial estate project in the Laguna-Batangas- Rizal area.

As usual, we met all sorts of unbelievable problems in this project, ranging from sudden reversals of permits to congressional hearings accusing me of committing the "mother of all land scams," and many others. There was a time when we thought our only clients would be the mosquitoes that filled LIIP at night.

But truth and faith ultimately prevailed. Today, the LIIP has been fully sold out to very enthusiastic investors and still more inquiries for sites keep coming in.

Let me note that LIIP is in the town of
Binan, which is at the entrance of Laguna Province coming in from Metro Manila.

And we have now started setting up STARWORLD, another industrial estate at the opposite end of Laguna Province, particularly the town of Calamba, which is also the border town before the resource- rich province of Batangas.

In effect, we have covered the entire Laguna Province, which we envision to be the start in a long series of industrial estates that will bring progress to the residents of many provinces in Luzon.

STARWORLD is another joint venture with Samsung. I am truly heartened by the dynamism and productivity of our partnership with Samsung.

The experiences I have mentioned constitute only a portion of the successful Fili- pino-Korean joint venture projects that are growing by leaps and bounds every day.

Noteworthy are joint ventures such as Samsung Mabuhay Corporation in electronics, Amkor Annam in semi-conductors,

Goldstar and LG Collins, and many others. Indeed, Filipinos and Koreans seem to have found good partners in each other.

We have briefly discussed the important lessons and events of the past. Let me now talk about urgent matters that will profoundly shape the present and the future not only of the Philippines and Korea but of the global village.

At this very moment, our nation is hosting the APEC Summit, a gathering of 18 world leaders with their respective contingents determined to push regional cooperation, bringing free trade to new heights of freedom by dismantling all protectionist barriers.

Timetable

The basic timetable agreed upon for full lifting of protectionist trade barriers is year 2010 for developed countries like the United States and Japan, and year 2020 for developing countries like the Philippines.

In effect, poor and backward nations are given only a 10-year "grace period" to attain the same level of market openness and competitiveness as rich and advanced nations.

The situation is made worse by the current administration's overly ambitious plan to fully open up the Philippine economy by year 2003.

To meet the 2020 deadline would already be miraculous considering that we are so far behind, both in virtue and the capabilities of our human resources as well as the harsh realities of running a business with limited resources. To think that we can make it by 2003 is, to my mind, unrealistic if not madness.

The supreme irony here is that the staunchest advocates of free trade would not have attained their present strength if they had not been highly efficient and effective protectionists in the past.

In a level playing field, free trade would be beautiful and would unleash our best potentials. But in a highly lopsided situation, the implications are obviously ominous, portentous of grave danger.

We should listen to all voices in our society, especially the voice of the weak.

What I understand is if APEC regional cooperation will indeed create the right conditions for shared growth and shared prosperity, then we should work for it, with it, in it, with all our heart and soul. We must be clear, though, on how shared growth and shared prosperity will be translated into our daily lives.

From the very founding of APEC during the inaugural ministerial meeting in Canberra in 1989, South Korea's role in APEC has been very influential, significant, and crucial. Given the great economic stature that it has already reached, South i Korea is now in the "rich nations" category in APEC. As a Filipino, belonging to a nation that is still poor and struggling for a place of dignity and identity in the global community, let me therefore use this forum to appeal to the rich-member nations of APEC such as South Korea, Japan, and the United States, to *help make world trade truly harmonious and fair.*

No free trade

Notice that I have avoided using the two most popular words in the APEC language: *"Free Trade."* Nothing is free in this world. Only God can give anything free.

Every person, everything, has a price or a condition to it. At most, trade can be harmonious and fair, but it can never be free. At the very least, let us be honest on the nature of trade.

Let us work together to build international trade that is harmonious and fair. This is my central message and appeal.

Harmony and fairness are related but not necessarily synonymous terms. There can be harmony without fairness, just as there can be fairness without harmony. We do not need the harmony and peace of the graveyard. We need harmony founded on fairness and justice.

Harmony and fairness can be attained only if APEC sincerely pursues trade on the basis of a just, fair, harmonious relationship among the participants. The strong nations play the dominant responsibility of inspiring and uplifting the less privileged by their actions of fairness, equity, and justice.

Otherwise, it becomes a farcical exercise that will benefit only the rich and strong nations. Poor nations will become even poorer.

Yin and _yang_

The very flag of South Korea, depicts the harmony and balance between *yin* and *yang,* the elemental forces of the universe. It sums up a people who live by interacting force that aims to meet at a balance state. It sums up a people who understand what it means, what it takes, to build a country where harmony and exist. It sums up a people with the courage and political will to do what is best for their country and people foremost.

In the same manner that joint venture projects between Filipinos and Koreans have been forged with expectations of mutually beneficial rewards, there can also be conflicts and differences arising from such ventures.

I believe, however, that so long as we keep on building in good faith and trust, there will be more successes.

Let the relationship be oneof authentic fair trade and equitable harmony.

Together, we will not fail in building trade that is harmonious, fair and beneficial to our common good.

Thank you.

XVIII The Missing Middle: Responsive Banking in the Next Millennium

General Membership Meeting of the Bank Admtnistration Institute, Philippine Chapter, The Peninsula Hotel, Makati City, January 30, 1997

Thank you for the invitation to speak before you today. I just returned recently from Geneva to speak before a conference of the United Nations Conference on Trade and Development (UNCTAD), focusing on enterprise development in the context of globalization and trade liberalization. Like the other participants, I drew many lessons from the experiences and insights of delegates from 185 countries. I got one of my important lessons outside the session hall.

Our blessed country

For five days I did not see the sunlight. It was all gray and gloomy the whole day through and I had to endure the stinging discomfort of frostbite from my nose to my toes. Such forbidding landscape only made me realize how beautiful and blessed our country is, with sunlight the whole year round, fertile soil, seas and rivers teeming with life, a warm, friendly, hospitable and talented people, and an abundance of natural riches.

The missing middle

The other lesson I learned was not entirely new. It has to do with what UNCTAD refers to as the "missing middle," that vast divide between a few large corporations on one end and numerous struggling enterprises at the other end.   .

Coming on the heels of that experience and being asked to speak about responsive banking in the next millennium, and considering my own background as an entrepreneur, I am therefore inclined to speak about the plight of the small and medium enterprises, the "missing middle."

I will not dazzle you with statistics about the potential contribution of small and medium enterprises to national development. You probably already know your figures about that. Let us also not dwell on through and I had to endure the stinging discomfort of frostbite from my nose to my toes. Such forbidding landscape only made me realize how beautiful and blessed our country is, with sunlight the whole year round, fertile soil, seas and rivers teeming with life, a warm, friendly, hospitable and talented people, and an abundance of natural riches.

The missing middle

The other lesson I learned was not entirely new. It has to do with what UNCTAD refers to as the "missing middle," that vast divide between a few large corporations on one end and numerous struggling enterprises at the other end.

Coming on the heels of that experience and being asked to speak about responsive banking in the next millennium, and considering my own background as an entrepreneur, I am therefore inclined to speak about the plight of the small and medium enterprises, the "missing middle."

I will not dazzle you with statistics about the potential contribution of small and medium enterprises to national development. You probably already know your figures about that. Let us also not dwell on the importance of small and medium enterprises to nation building. Everybody seems to agree on that score too.

Just yesterday, I came across an article about how SMEs account for the bulk of the total investment target set by BOI. In that same article were strategies for enhancing the development of small and medium enterprises. Those strategies are virtually not news anymore. You hear them echoed and re-echoed in many fora from Manila to Geneva.

Identity crisis

In spite of the rhetoric, why is the "missing middle" so elusive and what roles do banks play in its discovery or total extinction? How do we make the missing middle happen?

During the UNCTAD sessions, there was a common view that the main factor hindering enterprise development, from Asia to Europe to Africa to North and South America, was the lack of credit support for entrepreneurs, especially SME entrepreneurs.

The reason is pretty obvious. SME's by definition suffer from a crisis of identity and size. They are too large of micro-lending, yet not big enough to stand the tests applicable to large enterprises. The typical small and medium entrepreneur could just about be your average neighborhood acquaintance. You find him in every trader, producer, processor, or service provider engaged in small enterprises.

Those in this category are a miserable lot. They are not rich nor do they have enough properties to raise the amount needed. Their needs are too big for micro-lending, yet small and unattractive to banks.

We find in this group those who are trying to supplement a regular salary (the business not big enough yet to warrant resignation or retirement), who just lost a job or is unemployable, who has no rich relatives, and has little or no collateral.

While they have the greatest potential to evolve into big businesses, being small or medium is also the most critical stage in enterprise development.

To get a quick loan these days, you either have to be very big or very small. It makes business sense to lend to the big ones and politically correct to the poorest ones. In both instances, there are plenty of photo opportunities and a lot of PR mileage.

I still remember calling up my bank for a 50 million pesos accommodation which I needed — and they granted — in minutes. I also remember plight of one entrepreneur, presumably a small entrepreneur, who had to sweat it over for three weeks for a P100,000.00 loan.

Timing is everything

The circumstances may be different but it is still something lamentable. I've often been called by such courteous accolades as "mega-entrepreneur," etc., but I was also small once.

I have probably been luckier than others in that I have been able to pay my bankers on time, established a good track record, and eventually was able to get credit on the basis of my character and signature.

But in hindsight, I still shudder at the thought of those times when I was at the brink of disaster. One unreasonable banker would have been enough to put me on the road to ruin.

I know of friends and acquaintances who never were quite able to cross that thin line separating success and failure.

In some of these instances, a loan released a day earlier, or a few thousand pesos more of unsecured credit, would have made the difference. For the entrepreneur, timing is everything.

Too bitter

The failure rate for small and medium enterprises is too bitter to contemplate.

I am sure I am one of the very few who succeeded and yet it does not make me feel special. I am sure there could have been countless Elena Lims out there who could have been just as successful, if not more so, if only credit were available when they needed it.

The proliferation of loan sharks and lending investors only point to the fact that there is a big sector out there needing help, and who, in desperation just about grabs any available credit, regardless of the cost hoping that tomorrow will be a better day; that someday they will be big, and creditworthy enough for the banks.

Efficiency experts

Reading your brief history, I can see that you are an elite group of efficiency experts. You have practically perfected the way your operations are managed, finding the most effective and efficient way of doing things. I congratulate you for that.

The world of banking has really changed in the last few years, especially with the new technologies now available to you. I can see for example how it is now possible to move funds all over the world in milliseconds. Even demand letters and foreclosure proceedings have evolved into an art form.

With the advent of globalization and liberalization, you are also probably feeling the pressure from the entry of foreign banks. With many banks serving the same, limited clientele, one wonders whether the policy will harm existing banks who are already doing well.

Please help SMEs

If we seek to have responsive banking in the next millennium, I cannot see how you can improve further on what you are doing now in terms of operational efficiency. I think my message is clear that to be responsive, especially for the coming century, profits should not be the sole consideration. The responsive bank will be that which can make financing readily available to small and medium enterprises at such a scale beyond mere publicity, while at the same time protecting the interests of, and returning a fair profit to, its stockholders and depositors.

There are opportunities in this area which may require innovations in the way financial and management advisory services could be delivered to SMEs. It is important, however, that as much as the entrepreneur himself, the prospective financier must also have the entrepreneurial spirit.

Entrepreneurs think and act differently in many ways that may not be understood by your ordinary bank manager or analyst. Nothing comes close to the anxieties and tension of the entrepreneur. Meeting the next payroll, paying suppliers, bank loans maturing, checks bouncing, delivery schedules to meet, quality control, employee unrest, inadequate insurance, government bureaucracy, and so many other daily and strategic concerns all combine for a nerve- wracking experience that most people can never imagine.

Missionary

I used to say that an entrepreneur is a social worker. I have to correct myself. In truth, an entrepreneur is a missionary. Blood, sweat, and tears litter the very road he must travel in the development of enterprise. Such enterprise could collapse without the enabling environment to make it work, an environment where credit is available at fair rates.

The structure, terms, form and content of financing arrangements may also need a whole new concept. There is need to review and rethink approaches to credit evaluation, the tools for analysis, and information gathering and validation. Emphasis may, for example, be given to potential risk analysis, personal background inves- tigatioh, and behavior prediction. Credit analysts should be re-oriented and trained in these new tools and approaches.

Management services and operations review should also become as much tools for the financier as they are for the entrepreneur, the former to better protect his exposure; the latter to ensure success and growth for the enterprise. All these will have to be done the most efficient and reliable way, at the least cost affordable to the entrepreneur while at the same time guaranteeing the safety of, and a return on, the investment of the financier.

I hope I have succeeded in sharing with you today some of my thoughts. Nothing arouses my passion more than the trials and tribulations of the entrepreneur. I am thankful to the banking community for helping me all throughout my entrepreneurial career.

If you were able to help one Elena Lim, I hope you could do the same for a million others, and I assure you we will then find the "missing middle."

Thank you and good day.

XIX CPAs in the Global Economy

General Membership Meeting of the Association of CPAs in Commerce and Industry; Skytop, Hotel Intercontinental, Makati City, February 20, 1997

Let me thank you first of all for the kind invitation to speak before you today. I have been making the rounds of the speech circuit recently, but this is one of those rare instances when I will be speaking before accountants.

There seems to be one common theme though in the topics I have been asked to speak on: globalization.

Not only is globalization the latest buzzword, it is also the most recent reality that will have the most profound impact on the lives of men and nations in the years to come.

It is no surprise therefore why everybody seems to be groping for his or her role in this new order. Everybody also seems to be willing to hear from just about anybody about what the future should be and will be. For me to even suggest what CPAs should do in a global economy in terms of technical preparation, research, or the development of principles will be a bit presumptuous. I can only tell you my expectations as a layman, or at least that of the entrepreneur that I am.

All throughout my entrepreneurial career, I have been dealing with accountants, from my own staff to our external auditors. I deem them a necessary part of doing business, a vital link to good business success. I know of several quite prosperous entrepreneurs who even regard their accountants as somebody handy only when the taxman comes along. That I think is unfair.

Saviors?

Accountants have always had a role in the global economy since accounting first started coming of age in the 1930's after Wall Street crashed in 1929. Globalization should be nothing new to you.

For today's talk, I brainstormed with a few of my accountant-executives and asked them exactly how they perceived their role in society to be. One of them startled me when he said, "We are the saviors of the world." He said it in all candor and conviction, as if he were in front of a liberating army marching to the rescue of a besieged city.

Consider the following: One American president once said that the business of America is business. It is also generally acknowledged that the American economy's impact on the rest of the world is tremendous; that if America coughs, the rest of the world will have pneumonia. If America's business is business, then business runs the world. And if the language of business is accounting, then accountants are saviors?

The logic may be twisted and the analogy pushed a bit too far. I think, however, it gives richly deserved credit to the role of accountants. You must realize though that your job is still subject to a lot of misconceptions. Some people still see accountants as "bean counters" or "number crunchers" and sometimes you have yourself to blame for it.

Accounting is a product of its environment governed by principles founded on logic, reason and general acceptance. You never prove your principles through scientific experiments in the laboratory, or by some mathematical formula.

Accounting principles and practices respond to changing times, political and economic conditions, and investors and creditor expectations.

By this measure, accountants are supposed to be the most dynamic, and animated creatures around. I am afraid, however, that there might be too much emphasis on numbers and keeping books in balance? that the overall objectives of financial reporting are sometimes lost in the undeserved emphasis on exactitude.

You should be glad that there are new technologies now available to relieve you of clerical work. No machine will ever replace accountants.

We still live in a world of scarce resources, and human nature will lead us to entrust these resources in the hands of the best, the brightest, and the most capable.

Information provider

As business grow, more and more of these resources from more and more people will be entrusted to a few select and capable individuals. In all these, there are financing, investment, and other economic decisions to be made and accountabilities to be measured.

These decisions cannot be made sensibly without information about economic activities of an enterprise. You should therefore look at your role from this perspective, that of an information provider. Information that is relevant, timely, accurate, and faithful. If you go by this general objective, you will never go wrong in trying to define your role and responsibility to society, and the values you must have and live by to be able to fulfill that role.

It is time to forget the almost 50-year old definition of accounting as the art of recording, classifying, summarizing, etc. If that is still the way you define accounting, then you are about to be extinct, because the computer has taken over.

The computer never sleeps, is mathematically accurate all the time, and is always in balance. You will be no match.

Modern accountant

If you are not of the extinct variety, then you must be the modem accountant.

The modem accountant should be a student of human behavior. Many accountants have been guilty-of concentrating on the technical aspects, for example, of administrative controls at the expense of their social and behavioral contexts. On the contrary, the ultimate criteria by which many accounting control system should be assessed is behavioral - that is how does it affect what managers and their subordinates actually do and how do such activities fit into overall plans and objectives.

You must therefore develop a sensitivity for human nature. Try to reach out and be more understanding the next time around, instead of immediately rushing to your procedures and administrative manual.

The modem accountant should also be a good communicator and must have the ability to convey his thoughts clearly. In addition to a critical mind, the accountant of the future must be able to relate not just to his internal environment (management and subordinates) but also with his external environment (stockholders, and general community).

Humanities

Take time to appreciate music, or a good play, a painting, or a good book. This will give you proper balance and can only lead to your development as a total person. The world of numbers and pressing deadlines can be pretty drab and lonely. So let your spirits be lifted and give yourself a break.

Think of the grandeur of the Lord's Creation and the entire universe move in numerical precision. Your work can be attuned to the beauty of nature where order fills every space. Your work precisely fills order in the space of business. It is a wonderful contribution to be an important part of the world of business. Thanks to all the accountants who make life beautiful to good business.

He must also have a sense of cross- cultural awareness. Accounting principles may have universal applications, but culture among nations will always be unique. In a global work setting, it will not be unusual to be working in a multi-culture environment.

As a parting personal message, I would like to see the modem accountant be more appreciative of the arts.

Do not certify to fraudulent statements. To do this would certainly redound to the ruin of your inner peace and conscience, but ultimately will then ruin the company and the country. Mark my words, even those companies which are titans in their fields, can be ruined when accountants purposefully perform wrong statements to color their financial reports. Worst, if accountants deceive the public too. The need for your services will be eternal and the occupational risks are pretty acceptable, provided you do not certify to fraudulent statements.

XX

Developing Women Entrepreneurs Under Globalization

Women for Women Foundation (Asia-Pacific), Regional Meeting, Manila, Philippines, February 22, 1997

I have talked on entrepreneurship on many occasions, touching on many areas, from development of the enterprise, the role of government, value formation, financing and human resource. Whatever theme I was expounding on, I could never suggest that entrepreneurship would be easy.

Today's is even more daunting. Entrepreneurship for women in a global setting is a double whammy!

All of us know that entrepreneurial success is not gender-sensitive. Out of many who set out to become entrepreneurs, only a handful succeed.

Not because of gender, but by virtue of so many other factors. In short gender does not guarantee success. However, in this world where women are still fighting for equality among men, gender may hasten failure.

We also know that surviving in entrepreneurship within one's own local confines is already a tall order for most entrepreneurs. Before she can even think global, there are myriad of local problems and pests to contend with. These problems could be anything from an unfriendly local civil servant, lack of facilities, technology, and credit, inadequate contacts and distance from markets.

Right questions needed

And so it is therefore that I do not attempt to present you with solutions today in this brief talk. We must be modest in our expectations but lofty on ideals and concepts. We need a conceptual framework on which to build the future. This conceptual framework necessarily forces us to accept certain realistic assumptions about what the future can be for women entrepreneurs.

At this stage, the search for the right questions to ask is probably the more difficult task. In this the infant stages of our organization, there already is a pressing need to establish our linkages. Ironically, it is far easier to link between major capitals of the world than it is to reach out to a village organization maybe just beyond the next comer.

I am glad to know that the next speaker can speak with authority about the Internet and all its wondrous possibilities.

There are many possibilities for entrepreneurship in cyberspace.

Start modest

But like what I said, we need to strengthen locally first before we can think global. I only hope that we shall never lose sight of the small, neighborhood associations of women entrepreneurs which may need access to a wide range of assistance possibilities.

As a modest first step, let us be strong at the grassroots. It is easy to think global but more difficult to act local. It is therefore my simple wish for Our organization to have its program focused. Let us strengthen first the local base. It may surprise us to know that it is not that simple. There will be many problems and issues to contend with. But if we can address them with focus, commitment, and dedication, every little step will go a long way towards eventual globalization. The issues and areas of concern are many and diverse ranging from skills development, family and child care, management, values orientation, and women's rights. But no issue should or group should be insignificant to be dismissed as not part of a global whole. With modest beginnings could come great endings.

XXI
Human Resource Factor: Catalyst in Sustaining Competitive Advantage

10th Conference of Employers Conference, Sheraton Perdana, Pulau Langkawi, Malaysia; March 7, 1997

Boon or bane

The ASEAN region, which is on the threshold of rapid development, has a vast reservoir of human resources at various stages of readiness and development. These resources could either be boon or bane, depending on how they are effectively managed.

People: End, not means, of development

Human resources development goes beyond a mere headcount, or an inventory of available hands. It encompasses the whole range of skills, trainings, motivation, aspirations, dreams, hopes, and po-tentials of human beings, both individually and collectively.

If we are only now rediscovering that people, as one author put it, are the end of, and not the means, to development, it is not too late to embrace this paradigm shift.

Indeed, human resources are as familiar and as analogous as, say, any other tool of production.

In a production-centered environment, it is not difficult to identify equipment and processes, or resources if you wish, in the search for the competitive edge. Whoever has the best raw materials, the state-of-the art equipment, or the most revolutionary process, almost always has the edge. To regard human resources in this light, though justified, may be a bit overly simplified.

Contradictions and complexities

Human resources have their own contradictions and complexities compared to other tools of, and inputs to, production.

In a world of scarce resources, there ought to be reason to celebrate population growth because human resources seem to be the only one the world will always have ' plenty of. A rapidly growing population can however be cause for concern.

It is perhaps with deference and respect that we refer to the human factor as a resource, and perhaps rightly so. If it is, then why should we be concerned with its apparent surplus, in the face of uncontrolled population growth? It is only because a large headcount does not necessarily translate to a competitive edge but may even be a burden.

It is not uncommon for any company or organization seeking the competitive edge to review resources, programs, and processes and look for ways to improve, innovate, and enhance. Human resources, to be a major factor for success, therefore, must necessarily undergo a similar process.

It is not enough to have an abundance of manpower which cannot add value, or even worse, become a burden to organizations. If human resources are viewed merely as numbers, they cease to be what they purport to be. Instead, it becomes the bane that may in fact only add to costs rather than competitiveness.

In this regard, HR, like any other resource, needs to be identified, developed, maintained, enhanced, reinforced, and above all, motivated. We must however be cautious in pushing the analogy too far.

Process or sell

As you know, any business, when confronted with a seeming oversupply of resources will see a need to redefine its products and markets. It will be confronted with a classic "process-or-sell" decision.

It knows that further processing will add value, while selling or dumping the excess resources outright will relieve it of the burden of oversupply. Unskilled and untalented labor would be our equivalent of such unprocessed resource.

When we have an abundance of these, human resources become a mere commodity. It pains me to discuss this because, as you all know, my country happens to be one of the biggest supplier of overseas contract workers. This is not what the competitive edge is all about. To have that edge means being a little better than competition.

If HR is the catalyst for maintaining that edge, it therefore means that the total formation of the individual should be at the forefront of corporate strategies.

The need for training and education is pretty obvious. Investments in training and development by companies have been increasing, and in fact has given rise to some sort of an "HR industry."

Unlike other capital investment decisions which could be evaluated through sophisticated management techniques and measures like internal rate of return, payback period, or return on investment, the returns on any investment in human resource development cannot be measured quantitatively.

Much wasted money

Many organizations have wasted money on dubious HR programs.

It is virtually impossible to construct a list of development goals and techniques, but a few basic principles apply if the human resource factor is to be a major catalyst in maintaining the competitive edge.

People must be competent. Competence is the sum total of a person's education, values, and commitment to the organization.

More than the training programs that an organization provides, it has the bigger responsibility of clearly defining its mission and vision, its direction and purpose.

Any organization which fails in this should not expect to develop people who are competent.

The clarity of an organization's purpose should cascade to its human resources if it expects commitment to that purpose.

Purpose of organization: Basis of values

The purpose of the organization, its mission and vision, form the core around which corporate values, and eventually, the values of each individual member, are formed.

An organization, for example, which does not value innovation, should not expect its employees to innovate.

If the sense of purpose is clear, people- development will revolve around that purpose.

A focused company will not have difficulty defining its products and its markets, and therefore will be better able to match its human resources with those.

Under these circumstances, human resources development should be able to contribute to expanding existing markets, or reducing costs, or both. This is the least the human resource factor can do to contribute to competitiveness.

There are countless ways to contribute, it all depends on whether a culture is built inside a company which encourages such conscious and deliberate efforts by managers and employees.

Develop culture with feel for bottom line

The consuming desire to eliminate waste, or develop new products, or explore new territories, is almost like a religious crusade in many great companies, pervading even the lowest levels of the organization.

Among other things, therefore, there must be a culture with a feel for the bottom line.

Companies committed to building a reputation and a corporate character based on a proven track record of success, fairness, and integrity, will also most likely succeed in developing a competitive manpower base.

Business success is premised on sound business practices, both in theory and practical application.

Successful businesses, or at least those committed to become one, adhere to these practices, and in so doing will make mistakes. They however learn from these mistakes.

Proper delegation

An environment which encourages boldness, initiative, and decision-making sharpens the individual's competitive edge more than anything else.

Such environment is not possible unless there is proper delegation, mutual trust, and faith on capability of individuals.

The human resources of an organization will never be hardened enough if they cannot think and decide on their own.

Some companies lose the competitive edge because decisions, ideas, and initiatives were left to the exclusive domain of a few individuals.

A company wanting to maintain the competitive edge must also be wary of the dangers of perception versus reality.

The quality of human resources can be expressed in many ways and its attributes can at least be described qualitatively. Some attributes are more important than others in meeting the organizational objectives and it is the organization's responsibility to recognize these clearly and unequivocally.

For example, is creativity more important than flexibility? Once an organization identifies the attributes it considers important to its goals, it must determine how pervasive or lacking the attribute is in the organization.

These may be a matter of perception, in some cases. There must be overwhelming evidence in practice and actually contributing to organizational goals. Otherwise, there will be a wide gap between perception and reality, resulting in missed opportunities and unclear HR focus.

The HR specialist should be given management's total support in documenting research and obtaining empirical evidence in pursuit of HR development.

The organization's human resources can no longer be viewed in isolation as if they matter only while within the confines of an organization. They still do even if they are in their homes and families.

Beyond the company

In this light, the responsibility of an organization towards human development extend beyond its immediate corporate environment and into the community. It will be to the organization's best interest if its people go home to safe communities, or have access to day-care centers and health facilities for the children.

Companies will necessarily be involved in other emerging issues like the role of women, health, and education for the marginalized, and the plight of the disabled.

Unless companies and government act, some sectors may remain "unprocessed," and therefore not add value to the overall environment. In that scenario, there will be a surplus of unwanted commodity, ready to be dumped somewhere, at any price. It is not a pleasing scenario, but one that is already here and now in some areas of the world. You see this is in every beggar, in every street child, in every homeless person, even in every underpaid laborer.

Such a society is hardly the environment business is supposed to thrive in. The competitive edge definitely starts with the human resources, and we all have a role in its development.

XXII

Fostering Supporting Industries and RP-Japan Mutual Cooperation

19th Joint Meeting, Philippine-Japan Economic Cooperation Committee, Shangri-la Hotel, Manila, May 17, 1997

Thank you for the invitation to speak before you today.

I have an opportunity today to speak on a topic that is a concern of entrepreneurs like me who are engaged in the production and marketing of goods requiring inputs from a variety of source, both local and foreign.

Today's discussion is very country- specific, that is we are talking of cooperation between Philippine and Japanese industries. I am also tasked, to talk specifically about supporting industries. On that basis, I assume that we are concerned with inputs that go into the final product. These very inputs are what the support industries should provide to the final producer at reasonable prices so as to make the final product competitive.

I will have to be honest that I did not come here today with something novel that nobody has ever thought of, especially when we address the issue of supporting industries.

Complementation and linkages

The very first things that come to mind are concepts such as complementation and linkages.

These are not strange concepts. We have seen programs, heard ideas, and actually witnessed attempts at developing support industries.

The question is how far have these programs succeeded? If there is still much to be desired, what better way is there to finally make it work?

I do not want to be naive and start believing that the development of support industries in the automotive, electronics and packaging industries will come easy. It can be achieved though if we could only stick to the basics.

I do not want to spoil your appetite for anything, but my experience tells me that there is a long way to go indeed as far as these things go. It is not for lack of brilliant ideas. We have an abundance of those.

Economies of scale

Any two-bit producer surely understands what economies of scale is all about.

It is about volume and being able to sell to as wide a market as possible. If this condition, and this alone, is present, we are half-way through the development of a mature supporting industry.

Towards this end, many proposals have been put forward, even implemented. We clearly see this in the automotive industry, where parts and other components manufacturing have achieved a fair measure of success. But then maybe only because of government fiat.

Could there have been a parts manufacturing industry in the automotive sector if government did not require so?

Going over some materials on the government's Backward Linkage Program which most of you are probably aware of, I cannot help but be impressed with the model, the analysis and the concepts. I do not think I could improve on it, as far as the concept goes.

Success factors

One of the success factors it mentions is the need for the program to be demand-driven. We could come up in this meeting with a hundred other schemes and concepts, but if market forces do not create a demand for their products, supporting industries will never flourish.

Many years ago, I ventured into the manufacture of tuners for television sets, a perfect example of a supporting industry.

My company offered a product significantly lower priced than comparable imports, with a potential domestic market way beyond its break-even point, and enough incentives to guarantee profitable operations under normal market conditions. That company lost money and eventually closed.

The potential market simply refused to buy our products, because these companies happened to have access to a similar product, under their own brand, produced in their home country or somewhere else.

That they had to pay higher to bring these products in was of no consequence. There simply was no demand for my product as far as the other producers are concerned.

Quality Control

Another critical factor is quality and technical excellence of the support industries.

Quality control of material inputs is a serious concern for any producer. For support industries to gain acceptability and spur demand, quality must be reliable at all times.,

Otherwise, these final producers are well within their rights to insist on sourcing from time-proven, reliable, and quality suppliers. Most often, these are from within the same organization.

To be demand-driven means being market-driven, that "is, a market willing to buy and a producer willing to supply. Which of the two exists today?

Between the two, I would say that the first should come ahead. This means willingness and commitment to patronize products available locally.

It also means a genuine commitment to develop such supporting industries through transfer of appropriate technology, the sharing of technical expertise, and access to a wider market.

Cooperation

I am hopeful that eventually that day will come. Cooperation is what this body is all about. To cooperate is about the best that this committee can do.

No company can be forced to accept products it finds inferior, in terms of quality, delivery, or price. There are therefore responsibilities for both the main industry and the supporting industry.

These generalities apply whether it be the automotive, electronics, or packaging industry. That I was asked to focus on Philippines and Japan makes me a bit guarded in my assessment. Japan is a major trading partner and I have my share of experiences with companies.

Let me admit immediately that with regards to the consumer electronics industry, the industry I am most familiar with, there is a big lack of supporting industry to talk about for reasons I have earlier pointed out.

The volumes are not there yet, although that is of minor importance compared to our' and the other manufacturers willingness to buy components assuming these were available locally.

For most standard and generic parts, the decision is pretty straightforward, as long as the quality is acceptable and the price is reasonable.

Standardization

Standardization then is also a key consideration. This can be achieved, again, through mutual cooperation among major competitors, without anyone necessarily losing the uniqueness and individual superiority of its individual brand or product.

I also came across a recent article about Japan's role in ASEAN, as envisioned by Prime Minister Hashimoto where he called for "broader and deeper partnership" between Japan and ASEAN.

Japan's investments in the Philippines increased three and a half times between 1993 and 1995. Its factories in the ASEAN region not only cater to the export markets but are producing for the home market as well. These developments could only mean increased volumes which will be conducive to the development of support industries.

However, selling to and among subsidiaries will not contribute significantly to the development of supporting industries in every host country. The ideal partnership should be one of sharing and patronizing, producing as much in the host country as possible.

With this commitment by Japan, I am confident that the Philippines-Japan Economic Cooperation Committee through its concerted efforts will finally attain full development of support industries.

XXIII
The Meaning of Development

1998 Regional Conference on the Economic Empowerment of Women in the Asia-Pacific Region, at the National Vocational Training and Development Center for Women, TESDA Complex, Taguig, Metro Manila, April 27,1998

Honored guests, fellow women from various Asia-Pacific countries, the gentlemen present who rightly deserve the title honorary women, good morning and welcome to our 2-day Regional Conference with 120 Regional Participants on the Economic Empowerment of Women in the Asia-Pacific Region.

I am honored to be made Chair of this Conference. Thank you for your vote of confidence.

Adding to the significance of this Conference is that tomorrow, we will also inaugurate this National Vocational Training and Development Center for Women, a historic landmark project which we are all very proud of.

We thank deeply the Government of Japan for its strong support for this project.

Development means expansion of choices

The 1994 UNDP-HRD Report defines human development as the process of enabling people to have wider choices.

This is what this gathering is all about: To discuss and find ways to enable people, in general, and women, in particular, to have wider choices.

For the world's people, poverty is the main factor which limits their choices in very basic ways, as basic as living or dying, being healthy or ill, educated or ignorant, employed or jobless, living in dignity or shame.

For the world's women, their choices are limited not only by poverty but also by patriarchal or male-oriented social structures, shaped and instilled in hearts and minds through the ages, in virtually all parts of the world.

The process of correcting these structures started only late in this century, and we still have a long way to go.

Bedrock

That we have dedicated this Conference to the economic empowerment of women in the Asia-Pacific Region must be underscored, for it is a fact that economic empowerment is the bedrock of political, social, and personal empowerment for every woman.

The Conference aims to achieve certain objectives, mainly, to promote the economic empowerment of women, to share best practices and experiences of various countries in the Region striving for women's development, and to further collaborate efforts of various organizations, both public and private, local and foreign through networking in any form.

Easter and Centennial

Today is the Monday of the third week of Easter. As Easter is a time for New Hope and beginnings for many blessings, let us keep faith with our aspirations for a new deal for the women.

The presence of many interested women participants in the Conference and the lectures and experiences that we will learn from our Speakers, Reactors, and Participants, will be blessing themselves.

There is some cosmic logic in the coincidence that we are holding this Conference just a few days before the Filipino nation chooses its new leaders on May 11, and less than two months before we celebrate the Centennial of the declaration of the Philippine Independence on June 12, 1998.

By the way, it is an indication of the immense issues we still need to resolve as a nation that even on the correct date of our independence, there is still heated debate.

. On one side are those who claim that June 12, 1898, is the right date because General Emilio Aguinaldo declared Philippine independence from Spain's colonial domination on said date in Kawit, Cavite.

On the other side are those who claim that July 4, 1946, is the proper date for Philippine independence, because that was when the United States government officially withdrew its colonial rule over the Philippines.

Proponents of this view argue that Aguinaldo's declaration in 1898 had no factual basis because the Americans immediately became our new colonial master.

Of course, our ancestors were not cowards. They waged a heroic war for national liberation from 1899 to 1913.

We must never forget that one million brave Filipinos gave up their lives during that war to free our nation. They sacrificed their personal safety and comforts, their very lives, for us, the present and future generations of Filipinos. Unfortunately, we were defeated in that war by the superior military and economic resources of the Americans.

The outcome of the two events I have mentioned — Easter and our Independence Centennial — will indicate to a significant extent the roles the women choose to play. Has choice been widely used? Has the meaning of freedom impacted into our soul to frilly understand that the freedom we seek is not superficially the freedom from want but the real freedom of choice as to which role our lives will take?

Freedom within us

The freedom is in our minds, hearts, and the actions we do in exercising such choice. You can take a course, you can learn, but the most important ideal can't be taught. It has to be original and it can come only from within ourselves.

It is my hope that the results of this Conference, including the directions for a five-year (1998-2002) Action Agenda on the role of this Center for Women, will help guide the new leaders of the Filipino nation in crafting the right environment and policies for Filipino women, such that when our nation celebrates its next 100 years, it will be in a society where men and women have become true partners in creating a world closer to the ideal of every person having as much choices as the other.

I am optimistic that this Conference with its highly qualified Speakers and strongly motivated and interested participants will bring equally good results to our fellow women entrepreneurs in the Asia Pacific Region.

As Chair, I now declare the Conference open!

Thank you.

XXIV
The Path of Entrepreneurship

1998 Regional Conference of the Economic Empowerment of Women in the Asia-Pacific Region, at the National Vocational Training and Development Center for Women, TESDA
  Complex, Taguig, MM; April 27,1998

Honored guests, heroic fellow women, equally heroic honorary women - our gentlemen friends who have graced this occasion - good afternoon.

Thank you for this opportunity you have given me to talk about "Women in Business: Entrepreneurial Development for Women." These are two subjects very close to my heart: Entrepreneurship and Women.

Key indicators

There are no clear figures yet on the number of Filipino women-entrepreneurs; in fact, developing such a database is one of the major thrusts of this newly-developed Center for Women. However, the level of entrepreneurial development for Filipino women can be gleaned from some statistics of the 1997 Philippine Human Development Report: women make up 32% of the self-employed; further, only 8.5% of corporate presidents are women. Interestingly, the same pattern is repeated in the government bureaucracy, with women occupying only 29% of the managerial or policymaking positions.

Worldwide, according to a series of studies conducted or analyzed by the Washington-based National Foundation for Women Business Owners or NFWBO, women-owned firms comprise between ¼ to 1/3 of the business population - but with the positive caveat that women-owned enterprises are growing faster than the national economy in many countries, and in not just a few but in all industry sectors. In fact, women are starting businesses faster than men. In the US, women-owned firms are increasing at nearly twice the national rate.

An indication of women's growing business clout is that in a 1997 IBM-sponsored study of 50 leading women entrepreneurs worldwide, it was found that collectively, the 50 women entrepreneurs generate 139 billion US dollars in revenue and employ over 150,000 people.

Not fast enough

From these data, one conclusion we can make is that while the tribe of women- entrepreneurs is increasing rapidly, we still have a long way to go to attain a level of parity or equality with our male counterparts. I would even say that we are not moving fast enough in developing entrepreneurship among women. We should have a greater sense of urgency, we should work harder to bridge the gap faster, considering the urgency of the basic problems women now face.

In a situation where women in Asia-Pacific countries and the rest of the world are generally disadvantaged in relation to men, whether inside or outside the home, whether in rural or urban settings, whether employed in the private sector or in government, entrepreneurship could well be the faster path to economic and social equality between women and men.

Opportunities in crisis

But even if I raise entrepreneurship as a positive option for women, I must also put in a word of caution. Entrepreneurship, whether the men or women, is not necessarily the better or easier or more lucrative alternative to employment. To a large extent, it depends on the prevailing economic environment.

In a time of economic depression, such as now, it may be best to have a regular job as our anchor against uncertainty.

On the other hand, it is precisely during times of crises that the numerous opportunities exist for the entrepreneur. If you have what it takes to be an entrepreneur - the guts, sharp mind and instincts required - then in good times and in bad, you will always find or create opportunities for yourself.

From my personal experience and observation, as well as from various studies made on the subject, the mortality rate of businesses is quite high. For every ten businesses that get established, eight or nine go bankrupt after the first years; many don't even last for a year.

How many entrepreneurs have almost lost even their shirts or dresses when their businesses went under? How many entrepreneurs have almost lost their minds worrying how they're going to pay their skyrocketing debts, how to survive cutthroat competition, how to increase their sales which seem to be dropping every minute, how to collect receivables from clients who are also going bankrupt?

Quite simply, it is much safer and easier to be an employee getting a regular 15-30 salary, than to be an entrepreneur worrying about where to get the money for payroll, rent, electricity, fuel, etc.

Winner takes all

Especially in this new regime of globalization and liberalization, entrepreneurs in poor developing countries have to contend with competition from the economic juggernauts of rich developed countries. I have heard many speakers speak of globalization and liberalization in various fora as though these were manna from heaven. But we should not allow our minds to be clouded by illusions.

It was only in one forum where, for the first time, I heard the statement of truth from a Japanese speaker. He said that under globalization and liberalization, "the winner takes all." That's what we should put in our minds. Not that the world is for small nations like us to conquer, but the painful reality that there will only be one winner who will take all. No, it will not literally be one nation which will win, but it could be a bloc of nations or large multinational companies.

I say this not to discourage us, but for us to see the clarity of truth and act accordingly.

To my mind, it is like pitting the well- fed, well-trained, well-paid, gigantic NBA champion Chicago Bulls against a *barangay* team from Cotabato, one of the poorest provinces in Mindanao, where they are now eating poisonous yams to postpone starvation.

Sure, it's the same basketball rules, the same court, the same ball, the same number of players, but will the Cotabato team have any chance of winning against Michael Jordan and his crew?

In the Philippine case, the tragedy in the comedy is that many of our leaders think the Cotabato team, in this case the Filipino entrepreneurs, can already compete against the Chicago Bulls or the multinational companies.

We have no objection to free trade and competition but it should be on equal and fair terms. The developed countries conveniently forget that they attained their present economic growth strength by first going through a period of protecting their local industries.

We in the developing countries are now where they were 40 or 50 years ago, and we simply need more time to develop our strength to compete globally. At this point, our local industries still need to be protected.

Unfortunately, the forces that shape the world's affairs are much stronger than the small voices like mine. But I believe that if enough small voices speak out, the world will soon listen.

More government support needed

As though globalization and liberalization were not enough problems for the Filipino entrepreneurs, another major problem is the very poor support given by the government to entrepreneurs. For all the rhetoric of every new administration regarding support to Philippine entrepreneurship, the reality is that until now, it is extremely difficult for small and medium enterprises or SMEs to have access to adequate credit for working capital or for expansion. The loan requirements, especially for collateral, are such that they almost seem designed to disqualify SMEs.

But if, after you have carefully considered the realities of entrepreneurship, you are still moved by enough entrepreneurial spirit to take the giant leap of faith, then by all means do so.

Go where the water is deep

There is a saying that "To reach distant shores, you must be willing to go where the water is deep." It is a saying most apt for entrepreneurs. For in the development of entrepreneurs, it is not so much the technical training that counts, although it's very important for you to know as much as you can about the business you're in. Rather, the most important thing is the intangible entrepreneurial spirit that will put your imagination and heart on fire, that will give you courage and strength to climb even the highest mountains and cross even the roughest seas as you pursue your entrepreneurial dream.

Actually, very few undertakings can compare with the exhilaration and sense of fulfillment you can get from entrepreneurship, especially when you succeed against
seemingly impossible odds.

Kita

For example, when I decided to set up Kita Corporation, manufacturer of Aiwa brand color TV, audio, and video products, in the Clark Special Economic Zone in Pampanga shortly after the volcanic eruption of Mt. Pinatubo in 1991, all my foreign partners and my managers and staff were strongly against my decision.

Aiwa executives made several trips from Japan to see me at my house to try to change my mind.

They all thought it was a very foolish decision. They could not understand why I should prefer to set up a major factory in the middle of a wasteland of ashfall and lahar, when we have a premier industrial estate of our own in Laguna, the Laguna International Industrial Park or LIIP, which has all the infrastructure and the telecommunication facilities needed, and is very near the comforts and entertainment spots in Metro Manila.

But against the advice I stuck to my guns because I felt it my duty to show faith in the brave people of Pampanga, my fellow Filipinos, in their most difficult moment, struggling to rise from the devastation wrought by Mt. Pinatubo that literally buried their homes, their farms and businesses, their dreams.

I cannot begin to tell you about the difficulties we encountered every step of the way, as we constructed the factory and made it operational. But later events proved me right, as Kita became the biggest exporter of the Clark Economic Zone, earning the country millions of dollars from exports to Japan, Europe, and the Middle East. But for me, the greatest joy is in the feeling of accomplishment against fearsome odds.

More than money

Over the years, I have had the numerous similar experiences...

Like when I pioneered the growing and marketing of the black tiger prawn, even though the Japanese market initially abhorred its black color.

Like when I waged a one-woman crusade to bring to the Philippines an affordable people's car, the Kia Pride, despite objections and manipulations of the Japanese auto cartel who were raking in huge profits from their monopoly of highly marked-up cars.

Like when I dared to build the Laguna International Industrial Park right after the numerous coup attempts against the Aquino government, when most of the other local and foreign investors were leaving the country because of its instability, such that for several months after we completed the project, we thought mosquitoes would be our only clients as no one wanted to set up any factory; and many other instances when I had to fight great odds as a Filipino and as an entrepreneur.

In all of them, the deepest joy was not so much in the eventual financial success, but in the feeling of victory over awesome obstacles, the realization of the true power of the heart and entrepreneurial spirit, the feeling of fulfillment at having done something significant and helpful to Philippine society.

In hindsight, I must say that I owe whatever I am now to entrepreneurship. It was through entrepreneurship that I grew from various small businesses such as selling tomatoes in the streets of Leyte as a child, renting out comic books to other children -which often meant I had to translate and act out Tarzan, Flash Gordon, etc., to my captive but paying young audience, being a waitress in our small family canteen, into being the President of Solid Group, Inc.

I never thought that being poor, a woman, a *"probinsyana, "* with no connections whatsoever to political or economic powers would be barriers to my dream of someday becoming a good entrepreneur.

On the contrary, these were assets in building a strong resolve to attain my dream as they built my character to be strong, decent, fair, with honest fortitude and much closer to God, my true Partner in my dreams!

No barriers

Thus, to every woman or man, from the countryside to the cities of our country and foreign partners, imbued with the entrepreneurial spirit of mutual respect and fairness, notwithstanding the risks, the dangers, the sacrifices that lie along the way of entrepreneurship, and yet still ready and willing to take the road less traveled, I say go and pursue your dreams. There are no barriers to your dreams except yourself.

XXV
All Issues are Women's Issues

Women's Business Council Philippines (WBCP), 1st Meeting ("Working Lunch") of WBCP's Founding Members, Manila Polo Club, Makati City, May 27,1998

Fellow women in business, good afternoon.

From eight founding directors in August 1997, today we have gained 18 additional new members. That's more than 200 per cent growth in less than one year. Not a bad growth rate at all but in absolute figures, we still have a long, long way to go.

To our new members, congratulations and welcome to the Women's Business Council of the Philippines.

Two propositions

You have just taken the brave and bold step of joining an organization dedicated to two propositions:

• First, all issues are women's issues, from birth to death, from the family budget to the national budget, from the economy to environment;

• Second, all men and women are created equal, entitled to the same basic rights accorded every human being at birth.

Vision

You have joined a council envisioned to be the "voice of Filipino women in business" in much the same way that the Philippine Chamber of Commerce and Industry or PCCI is the voice of business in general.

Towards the attainment of this Vision, the official Mission of our Council is to build a culture that is cognizant of women's contribution to the economy, and supportive of women's quest for excellence, whether as workers, entrepreneurs, owners, or executives, in pursuit of sustainable economic growth, competitiveness and social equity.

You have just accepted equal responsibility for the accomplishment of this Mission, and I am fully confident of the seriousness with which you will do the work involved.

Flagship projects

To concretize our Mission, we have four flagship projects:

*   First, Database Development, to ensure that we base our actions on timely and accurate data on women's concerns.
*   Second, the Women's Business Center, a one-stop assistance center for all women in business.
*   Third, the Entrepreneurship Program, meant to develop the capability of women as entrepreneurs through various training courses.
*   Fourth, Policy Advocacy, our proactive lobby campaign to influence our male-dominated Congress to come up with legislation beneficial to Filipino women in business.

However, I would like to suggest a fifth flagship project: Membership Expansion and Consolidation. After all, in a highly political environment, numbers often become the litmus test of organizational strength.

Thus we should intensify our efforts to gain new members, not only in Metro Manila but in Luzon, Visayas, and Mindanao.

Our freedom

The tremendous challenges we need to surmount can be gleaned from studies such as the 1997 Philippine Human Development Report, which reveal how women remain highly disadvantaged relative to men. For example, despite all the efforts to promote gender equality, until now women make up only 8.5% of corporate presidents and 15.4% of vice-presidents. The same pattern is repeated in the government bureaucracy, with women occupying only 29% of managerial or policy-making positions.

Whatever we accomplish this year relative to urgent women's issues takes on a special historical significance, in that we are celebrating the centennial of our nation's declaration of independence. After 100 years, it is high time for us Filipino women not only to earn our rightful place in history, but even more important, our rightful share in our nation's future.

To succeed in our flagship projects is to succeed in our Mission. To succeed in our Mission is to succeed in pursuing our Vision, which is to be authentic voice of Filipino women in business.

All issues are women's issues. Our freedom will be our nation's freedom.

Let us waste no time, then, in drawing this lofty dream close to reality.

Thank you.

XXVI
Information is Urgent Because Development is Urgent

Launching of Destiny Integrated Multimedia's CYBERTRONICS CITY; Pan Pacific Hotel, Manila; October 1,1998

The main question that concerns me is: What is the significance of Destiny Cybertronics City? What larger purpose is served by being able to deliver ever increasing amounts of information at ever increasing speeds? So what if today we can download 1,000 pages in ten seconds and tomorrow we need only a split-second? What good does that do us, as individuals and as a nation?

Reflecting on these questions, I realized that we pursue speed in communication not for its own sake. In the Information Age we live in, the key to a nation's development is information. Therefore, the urgency of the need to develop our information capabilities lies in the urgency of our nation's need to develop. Information is urgent because development is urgent.

200 Filipino children die daily

Development is urgent because each additional day of poverty is literally a life or death matter for poor Filipinos, especially the children.

According to UNICEF studies, every day more than 200 Filipino children die due to hunger and poverty-related diseases. Every day, hundreds more fall victim to mental retardation and physical impairment again due to malnutrition and poverty.

As one UNICEF official put it: "It is like fully loading one jumbo jet with Filipino children every day and then letting the plane crash." But unlike a plane crash, this daily tragedy does not hit the headlines because poverty is a silent killer. Its victims die separately, silently, and secretly.

Therefore, we urgently need to put a stop to this silent scourge. We must pursue speed in information to speed up development because one more Filipino child destroyed by poverty is one child too many. We must pursue speed in information to speed up development because development delayed, like justice, is development denied.

Information and'technology

Exactly how is information linked to development?

Exactly how can information help us in our war against poverty?

The answer lies in the role information plays in ensuring a nation's economic success, especially in this era of globalization and liberalization.

To succeed in today's global competition, you need to have accurate, and fast and timely information on where to find the best and suitable parts, products, technology, funds, skilled human resources for all needs, business or otherwise. He who gets first information is able to take advantage of the opportunities first. He who comes in late has to content himself with leftovers, more handicaps to catch-up.

The relentless campaign of First World countries for the strict and total implementation of Intellectual Property Rights or IPR, is proof positive of how critical the control, access, and utilization of information is.

The irony is they did not respect Intellectual Property Rights in the past to develop and strengthen their respective economies, and yet they are now prohibiting Third World nations from using the same strategies.

The greater tragedy is that instead of protesting against this patently unfair arrangement, many Third World leaders become the leading salesmen and apologists for globalization and liberalization, urging their citizenry to accept this new world order meekly, even gladly, on pain of economic sanctions by First World nations. Is this fair trade? Of course, not.

Affordable information

I see in Destiny Cybertronics City the affordable means through which Filipino students, from grade school to high school and college, in both private and public school nationwide, will develop computer literacy and become exposed to the latest knowledge and information via the internet.

Clearly, we cannot become competitive in the global business arena if our people, especially our youth, remain computer illiterates.

I can hardly wait to see brilliant creative energies that will be unleashed by the Filipino youth once they gain literacy and eventually mastery over computer and information technology.

I can hardly wait to see the new Filipino who will emerge as we are able to reach more of our children through the magic and power of information technology, orient them on the right values at an

early age, teach them the values of integrity, not corruption; love for country, not colonial mentality; love for their fellow human beings, not self-centeredness; hard work and pride in their work, not *"palusot"* (excuses) and *"puwede na"* (good enough); the value of enthusiasm, of always striving for excellence in whatever they do.

Above all, the value of faith, trust, and obedience to an all-loving God.

I see in Destiny Cybertronics City the means through which Filipino entrepreneurs, from SMEs to large corporations, will have affordable and cost-effective information tools to advertise their products and services worldwide at very low rates, source suppliers and potential business partners from a global pool, and be updated on the latest technology for their business needs.

I see in Destiny Cybertronics City the means through which technology will change our lives for the better, totally redefining our traditional ways of living, working, and playing.

Comic books

Such a view of the future may seem like just a wonderful dream now, but I am a firm believer in the power of dreams, the power of daring to dream and having the courage to act to make the dream come true.

As a child of nine in Tacloban, one of my first entrepreneurial activities was renting out comic books for a few centavos to our neighbors. Since many of the children in our neighborhood couldn't understand English, I gave the value-added service of being a one-girl theater, telling the stories of Flash Gordon, Mandrake the Magician, Tarzan, Superman, and other superheroes in Waray, the local dialect, along with sound and special effects even the creators of those heroes couldn't have imagined in their wildest dreams.

Looking back, I realize that was my first taste of multi-media presentations.

Looking back, I realize that was my first step in the enterprise of building human relationships, which became the common thread running through all the businesses I eventually got into, from consumer electronics, black tiger prawns, industrial estates, the people's car, and now integrated multi-media through Destiny.

Pursue the vision

All these started as dreams and I have seen in my lifetime how I have actualized these dreams.

It is with vigor in my faith, enthusiasm in my soul, energy in my mind and in my body that I pursue this dream. The dream has become an actuality in the vision of my son, David to create the Destiny Cybertronics City in a spirit of integrity and Godly values.

That is why I would like to invite you to join me in the dream to use the power of information to speed up our nation's development.

In closing, let me share with you the Vision we are pursuing through Destiny:

In today s Information Age, information is the key to development for individuals, families, and nations. An informed people is an empowered people. To speed up access to information is to speed up development. To democratize access to information, to make it accessible to even lower-income groups, is to democratize development, making it real and meaningful to the many, not just the few. In brief, to democratize information is to democratize.

To speed up and democratize access to information for the Filipino people. This is the Vision of Destiny.

Please join us in pursuing this Vision.

XXVII
East Meets West: Tapping Marketing Aptitude

10th Annual Marketing Educators'Conference; Philippine Trade & Training Center (PTTC), Manila; February 21, 2000

The subject I am assigned to speak on is "International Trade / East Meets West: Tapping Marketing Aptitude."

At the onset, let me say that what I have to speak is not the rhetorical, scientific, methodological aspect of marketing, be it East or West aptitude, but my own experiential process.

I suppose that's why you have asked me to speak on this subject: I have personally lived through the journey of practicing the process of doing international trade from importing, manufacturing, servicing and exporting, which includes all facets of marketing activities.

Perhaps, this experience makes it my comparative advantage over some of you who have only read and studied business from the books.

Let me say that the East and West syndrome is not relevant to today's world of globalization. The demarcation line between East and West is fast disappearing and in some regions of the world it has disappeared. Think of Eastern Europe before and what it is today.

The walls of Berlin have been demolished and the Eastern bloc is now open to the world.

In Asia, many countries have folded into the Western marketing syndrome and can no longer be isolated as the undeveloped East as against the developed West. Japan, Singapore, Hong Kong, Korea, Taiwan, and coming up, China, are such examples.

The closed economy and protection concept of the past is steadily and surely melding the East and West.

What seems to be looming in the future would be a world market dominated not by the East or West standard, but by the superiority of technology, infrastructure, products, management, country governance and people's development.

On Technology:

The 3rd millennium is a technology millennium. Think of the far-reaching power of the internet in moving goods and services by the mere click of a mouse.

Today, you can order books, cosmetics, sporting equipment, appliances and trade stocks, simply by turning your computer on and clicking a few keys and *voila!* - you have consummated a business transaction.

It is also true with search for information and exchange of ideas at unlimited time and speed. The countries that have the more advanced technology will sweep the market. U.S., Australia, Japan and Singapore are ahead in this race.

Scoreboard says: The developed countries will have the edge because they have the massive infrastructure to support the technology.

The developing countries have yet to be "wired," a David and Goliath battleground, except that David does not even have a slingshot.

Even a telephone is sorely lacking. Per ratio, we have 80.7 telephone lines for every 1,000 Filipinos. That's how poorly connected we are.

On Products:

Sophisticated products with advanced technology dominate the market. We can only hope to provide the services ranging from OCW technology to manual labor type export operations (of course, commendable too, but with low technology transfer and rather small percentage of social impact); some local products with market niches also help.

On Management, Country Governance, and Human Development:

Best business practices are deemed to be adopted by both East and West marketers, this should be a common value to all. But management techniques, strategies, policies, etc. also require high education, knowledge and information-adequacy, technology and infrastructure adaptability, good country governance and transparency, and most of all, investment in human resource development. They are all interlinked like a chain of strength. A weak link is enough to break the chain.

Dear friends, as I've gone through several miles of entrepreneurial journey likened to an ascent of a small mountain near Mt. Apo (reported to be the tallest mountain in the Philippines scaling over 10,000 ft. above sea level), it was still a hurdle of some kind of obstacle course.

This is not to discourage you but to strengthen your nerves to what's in store for one who would hurdle the East-West or North-South borders of business, specifically in the marketing area.

It can also bring satisfying rewards where you feel you have competed, made your mark, contributed to the growth or even maintenance of your markets under an environment of integrity, decency and fair play.

Prawn export

As a small example, let me cite my experience in the development of the export market of the Philippine black tiger prawns.

As early as the seventies our company pioneered the processing and export of these prawns found in many of our fishponds.

There was no market for this specific specie of prawns because of its blackish appearance and unfamiliarity to both the East and West markets. But because of our firm conviction that this black tiger prawn was even more delicious than the normally accepted prawns caught from the sea, we went into a marketing campaign that brought down all the biases and prejudices against our Philippine indigenous prawns.

First, we attacked the nearest market — Japan. We entered into marketing arrangements with the Japanese wholesalers to promote our prawns.

Good negotiations, fair deals, and mutually beneficial cooperation brought about the birth, growth, and prosperity of this lowly product which eventually influenced the West to accept this commodity even at a premium price aside from stirring our Asian sisters to likewise go into this business.

In brief, marketing aptitude between East and West can be melded so long as it is anchored on integrity and human values of fair play.

What I'm saying here is that we can observe the differences in the culture and in the way or manner of marketing relationship between the people or their companies, but if in the final analysis what will prevail is the due respect and fair relationship of each party, it will matter little on the geographical or racial difference. **Arrogance and greed**

Unfortunately, in this imperfect world, many soured relationships grew from the unfairness and arrogance of the stronger party over the weaker one.

I think this aptitude is inherent in man's greed for one to beat the other, although fully knowing how unfairly one has been behaving.

Take the case of many take-over or mergers of companies that have been affected due to globalization. The dominant party swallowed the lesser party in gaining expansion of his world market without giving due respect or strengthening the market in its area of jurisdiction. This has caused much heartache and unfavorable consequence in the business relationship.

The realities of today are no longer the countries of East-West or North-South competition for world domination. Market competition is a free for all. Who produces the best product at the most competitive price and delivers within the quickest time is the global winner.

In such a background, it is really a struggle for winning the gold by developed countries against developed countries, and not developing countries, or a strong developed company against its peers.

WTO reforms needed

The Seattle World Trade Forum last year precisely collapsed because of the perceived inequities and imbalances prevailing among the developed economies and the undeveloped economies.

A great segment of the protestors came from the developed economies, US to begin with, when its own constituents protested against their fear of losing their jobs and security.

Recently, European Union Commissioner Lamy in his address to the European Parliament urgently called for the resumption of the World Trade Forum and ask for the resolution of two key obstacles, namely:

• Address the needs of the developing countries within the WTO (156 member-countries); and
• Institute reforms in the WTO process.

Developing countries complain of many glaring imbalances and unjust implementations within the WTO Agreements.

They look with suspicion on the WTO that is under pro-developed country leadership.

This is quite natural because the greatest fear of developing countries is to be further marginalized and reduced to further indignity in their lives because of their inherent limited resources and capabilities.

Reduced to mere consumers

Take a look around you - see what we eat, drink, consume, wear, read, study, etc. etc. We have been reduced to mere "consumers," no longer producers. Is this our legacy to our children?

Our country is in great deficit - we cannot balance our income and expenditures. We continue to be more debt-ridden year by year. And more jobs are lost. We are driven to work overseas as migrant workers. The grass in our pasture cannot support us anymore. We need to do more trade on goods and not on people. But beyond trade, we need to be productive producers ourselves and not be mere importers and consumers. I often hear a common remark from our foreign partner, "The Victor/Winner takes all." Isn't this ominous?

Before this happens, there is a need to rationalize global trade. It must be anchored on human development where all nations, both developed and developing, will prosper.

Hypocrites

U.S. President Bill Clinton in the World Economic Forum last month in Switzerland said:

"Let me be as clear as possible on this. We shouldn't do anything to stunt the economic growth and development of any developing nation. I have never asked any developing nation, and never will, to give up a more prosperous future. But in today's world, developing countries can achieve growth without making some of the mistakes most developed countries made on worker protection and the environment as we were on our path to industrialization."

Let me cite Jesus in one of his teachings to the Pharisees and scribes who always spoke with authority of their righteousness. Jesus responded: "Hypocrites — these people honor me with their lips, but their hearts are far from me."

It's easy to say that developing countries must prosper with the developed countries. Unless the hearts of the developed countries are in their deeds - they help the people in the developing countries attain a decent and humane life by not marginalizing them under today's creed of globalization.

Globalization for the harmony and peace of all, dispersal of concentrated wealth to reach the bottom poor (entitlement to education, healthcare, housing, livelihood, jobs, etc.) and not to be "gobbled" into further poverty.

In the Philippines, the present globalization situation puts us in the *"alanganin* (indeterminate) middle." We are behind our ASEAN brothers, Thailand, Malaysia, Singapore, and even Myanmar and Vietnam are fast catching up. Should there be a debt-relief forthcoming, we will not be included because this will be for the poorest of the poor nations only.

Yearly, we are faced with the same problems. They never go away but they become more intense. Look at our poor infrastructure, rutted and patted roads, inadequate transportation, uncollected garbage, floods, traffic jams, squatters, deterioration of education, unemployment, etc. The deficit is getting bigger. We spend more than what we earn. Yet, what we spend on have not really improved the lives of the bottom poor.

We must do our share

This looks like a gloomy picture. But the phenomenon is that despite the problems mentioned, the economy is improving. Central Bank has stabilized the currency and interest rates. Agriculture is now being made a priority program. Education is undergoing reforms (more books and school buildings and improved curricula).

Slowly but surely, we are moving forward, although not as fast as our ASEAN brothers who are doing better. This should be a cue for all of us to do our bit. All of us have a stake.

We can shout, criticize and throw bricks, or we can do more positive actions like making the necessary reforms in all government sectors (fight graft and corruption) promote peace and order, provide more jobs, import less unnecessary consumables, educate our children to aspire for knowledge and skills, and above all, live and practice good ethical values for love of country and people, evermore.

XXVIII
LMCP: A Vision for the Third Millennium

Inaugural speech as incoming President (2001) of the Legal Management Council of the Philippines (LMCP); Manila Polo Club, Makati City; March 5, 2001

I am honored by this confidence you have given me to serve as your President. To all my fellow members, both new and old, join us as we move the LMCP forward into the third millennium.

We stand on an immense mountaintop built on nearly two

hundred thousand years of human existence. To recall, earliest fossil records indicate that the human species, *homo sapiens,* first appeared in Africa about 195,000 years ago.

As human beings, as Filipinos and as members of the LMCP, we cast our eyes on the richness of our history and the great responsibility it places on our shoulders. Our responsibility is to take this history and knowledge, particularly in our legal profession, turn around, take in the view the mountaintop gives us and chart our course into the future.

Help stop slavery

Our countrymen deserve the fullness of respect.

In this context, it is the LMCP's duty **to strive to promote legal and government processes that will prioritize and support Filipino small and medium sized enterprises.** History places its hand on our shoulders and we must respond.

, Too long have we as a people sent out wave after wave of our children with misguided pride, to become bonded slaves in foreign lands.

For lack of local opportunity and spurred by the greed of manipulative institutions that only look at dollar remittances, the best of our youth leave, supposedly to help their families, but more often than not come home to broken families and social disorder. What can we do about this, you may ask.

We must bring our people home. Our highest priority is to build a new economic system that will enable them to use their talents and expertise here, build their businesses here, and raise their families here.

Support Filipino SMEs, not MNCs

The LMCP is a Filipino institution and it must promote Filipino business, through consultancy and advocacy, helping other institutions, particularly government in streamlining procedures, allocating incentives, and providing protection from unfair competition.

We must end our inexplicable slavish attitude that places multinational corporations (MNCs) and selected big businesses on a pedestal with the lion's share of support. They are not the ticket to national progress and prosperity. They never were and never will be.

The truth is that the majority of our nation depends on Filipino SMEs (small and medium enterprises) for their daily income, survival and hope for the fixture.

The SMEs are the true engines of our nation's economic and

cultural rebirth. I say cultural rebirth as well because it is through supporting the growth of Filipino SMEs that we will win back our sense of national pride and self-sufficiency and show an example to our youth.

Common good above legal

What is our vision as we stand on the mountaintop? What is it that we must seek?

Let the LMCP hold up a torch not of what is legal but of what is relevant to the common good of our people.

Let us stand with our government at all levels and assist through consultancy and advocacy, a review of procedures and processes that affect our Filipino brethren in business, to redesign them to promote and protect them every step of the way.

Let us work with financial institutions to work out solutions that will answer their needs instead of forcing them to try to meet impossible standards that only big businesses can meet.

There is much we need to do my friends but we must rise to the task with fidelity and urgency. The eyes of the future generations are upon us. Let us work with righteousness and goodness in our hearts so that one day, the generations to come will stand on their mountaintop and gaze on the richness of their inheritance and see us here today in LMCP and be proud to be Filipino with us.

God bless you all and thank you.

XXIX
Lessons from Comic Books

Excerpts from Welcome Remarks at the 2nd Asia Pacific Business Convention and Exhibition on Globalization and Transformative Leadership; "Men and Women in Business: Partners in the New Economy," Hotel Intercontinental Manila, Makati City, March 19, 2001

I feel compelled to speak to you today about... comic books. You see, as a young barefoot girl in my province after World War II, I had a small but thriving business of renting out comic books to the neighborhood children.

But the business really picked up when I offered to read to the ones who didn't know how to read. And I did so complete with full emotion and actions. You might say I was a pioneer in the field of multimedia technology.

While it did not become my lifelong career, my stint as the

neighborhood's chief storyteller instilled in me certain values that are true today.

Let me illustrate:

Value 1: Help people overcome limitations.

Everyone has his or her limitation. Some cannot read comic books while others cannot plan a business beyond today's collection. Our businesses or services are truly valuable when they help a person see, understand and reach beyond what she normally can. Let our business activities not be focused on products and services but on raising people's **quality of being** and not just quality of living.

Value 2: Make opportunities within.

Despite all our hardships at the time my whole family was committed to making things work where we were. No talk of leaving for another country or looking for handouts. We buckled down and made opportunities where we could - including the comic book interpretative readings. Our business efforts must make opportunities here and not join the mad scramble to go abroad. I am always saddened by the misguided pride some people, even in government; take in citing the growing numbers of Filipinos abroad. They never count the social cost on their families and eventually our very society. Let us use this convention to develop opportunities within for all respective communities.

Value 3: Give everything.

My comic book business would never have prospered if I didn't give one hundred percent every time I read for my young, excitable, poor audience.

Hands flying, eyes wide open, voice full of emotion, I became a live comic book for many of them. It's only when you give your all that people see your sincerity and give you their trust. It's only when people give you their trust then you can give them products and services that they really need. I urge all of you present to give a hundred percent of yourselves if you want to convince those you serve that you really care about being responsive and relevant.

Commitment is the beginning of Relevance. I have spent my life struggling as a teacher, lawyer, businesswoman, wife and mother and through it all, these values remain the same. I urge you to share these values with me as we go through this convention together so that we may leave it not just as successful businesswomen but as gifts to the communities we live in.

God bless you all and may this be a fulfilling convention for all of us.

XXX
Lessons from Poverty

Acceptance Speech on the Awarding of the Madame Helen D. de los Santos Memorial Medallion of Honor and Scroll of Commendation The University of Manila; March 31, 2001

Many years ago I was a little girl from the poor side of Tacloban, Leyte. I used to carry a thick bamboo stick over my shoulder with two kerosene cans filled with water hanging on either end. After doing that, I had to help with the chores in the house and ran errands for my young, widowed mother, delivering shoes and slippers and collecting payments around the neighborhood.

As you can see, all those heavy cans of water may have built my character but may have somewhat limited my height.

I am thankful for being chosen as this year's recipient of the Madame Helen D. De Los Santos Memorial Medallion of Honor. But I take it as a responsibility to share with all of you the compelling values that were planted in the heart of that poor little girl in Tacloban and guided my life.

Lesson 1: We Need Role Models.

We need to see and experience people who are willing to be living examples of timeless good values. My mother is my role model. She showed me how to be frugal, hardworking but fair to all people. She showed me and not just told me, that living good values was more important than making money or garnering honor.

The tragedy of our country is that it is not so easy to find good role models.

Many fathers and mothers are too busy making money to show their children how to live good values.

They spend less time to communicate with their children as the latter spend more time indulging in various distractions of the day such as watching TV and playing video games. Such activities do not enrich the mind and soul.

Most political leaders spend so much time tearing each other down, making us more confused and distrustful of their motives. Likewise, many religious leaders are under a cloud of cynicism, often suspected of ulterior motives, too.

From my humble experience, I have never, never made any celebrity, especially politicians, movie actors, sports champions, business tycoons, religious pastors, preachers, etc., the object of my role model to follow.

I look into the hearts of those who gave me life, sacrificed and toiled for my upbringing, who excelled in humility and love, as my shining role models.

Look to those who loved and protected you as your role models. You will never go wrong. Find a role model whose life is a witness to moral and social commitment, understand the values he stands for, and consciously apply them to your life. Viewing life from the perspective of a good role model will lend his wisdom to you and you will pursue your goals with the benefit of his life experience. And one day, you will find yourselves the role models for a generation to come. Do not let them down.

Lesson 2: Value is in sacrifice

The foundation of all success is not intelligence but sacrifice. Rudyard Kipling put it so well when he said, "Humble because of knowledge, mighty by sacrifice!"

My own life, every step of progress I have had, has been built on sacrifices. Not just my own, but sacrifices of the many men and women, family and friends, who stood by me and paid the price alongside me.

I could stand with pride and deal with the biggest foreign businessmen, even those who looked down on women in business, because I stood on our blood, sweat and tears, our sacrifices.

And more often than not, our business was concluded successfully because they too respected our foundation of sacrifice.

Nothing valuable is built unless someone is willing to sacrifice for it. Nothing lasts unless we learn to be thankful for the sacrifice. If I am to inspire anything today, I pray it is to move you to embrace sacrifice rather than shortcut If enough of you here heed this call, then hope is alive for the future of this nation.

Lesson 3: Discern the essential

Time is the most precious resource. A successful life is one that recognizes that time is so valuable that we must apply judicious care in discerning what is truly essential to us, what brings forth life from the deepest recesses of our hearts.

And the essential is what allows us to uplift the **quality of being,** and not just quality of living, of our fellow Filipinos.

Every business I ever went into was examined first by what impact it would have on the life of my countrymen, especially those with less in life. I always strove to uplift their minds and souls as well as meet their daily physical needs.

For wasn't it Carl Jung who said," **the sole purpose of human** existence is to kindle a light in the darkness of mere being." Find what is essential and success will follow.

I have spoken enough. It is time to prepare your hearts to embrace the challenge of your lives.

Find the role models that you will need to build your futures. Rejoice in your times of sacrifice because you know you are building something that will last. Discern what is essential in your life. Recognize God's gift to you that enables you to become the light to the darkness in the lives of your fellowmen.

XXXI
On Time

Acceptance of Award for Punctuality & Civility Annual National Maagap Awards Organized Response for the Advancement of Society, Inc. (ORAS); Quezon City Sports Center , September 28, 2001

I am honored that the Board of Trustees of ORAS has given me this award for promoting the values of punctuality and civility. These values have been my faithful companions through the years and they have guided the way I have done business and lived my life.

Let me begin by quoting a line from my book, "Business in the Real World": *"Courtesy extended to superiors is called appropriate decorum; if extended among equals, it is civility; but courtesy extended to subordinates is nobility."*

It comes natural to me to give courtesy and respect to all God's people, big or small. But I have found that I am especially blessed when I am able to impart that respect to those the world takes for granted. The needs of the daughter of my driver merit the same consideration and time from me that any manager would receive from me as well.

In fact, there was an occasion where I personally corrected an HR manager who scheduled interviews with an applicant and repeatedly failed to meet the applicant, wasting her time and travel money. Civility becomes nobility when we extend it to those who are least able to demand it.

Punctuality, on the other hand, is also the fruit of respect for others. I am keenly aware of how busy people are and how difficult it is to travel so I make it a point to respect any effort to meet me by being on time, in fact always early for any appointment. If we truly respect people and want to show it, then we will value their time and effort and live the value of punctuality.

My friends, the true measure of every generation is the kind of people it produces. Unfortunately, this generation has started to forget that we must mold men and women who will uphold these values of punctuality and civility as a sign of a deeper value, a strong sense of respect for our fellowman and a concern for his welfare. I support the efforts of ORAS to revive the awareness and commitment to live these values as a stepping-stone to strengthening our Filipino culture and society.

Thank you and God bless us all.

XXXII
The Promises We Made

Speech before the Manila Bay Breakfast Club; Casino Espahol, Manila; October 12, 2001

At 72 years old today, I have lived virtually all of my life in the Philippines. Learned ABCs and basic values from childhood from my young widowed mother, worked through night courses in college and learned more ABCs - blue collar jobs - all in the Philippine environment. It sufficed for me. I've never studied abroad nor owned a square inch of land abroad, nor worked abroad, nor own any account abroad. It is with pride and thanks to God that all the ABCs and values I've imbibed in our country were more than enough to fulfill me.

After more than seven decades of my life, I can say that I've lived in very exciting times of Philippine history. I've gone through the years from the adoption of the Philippine Commonwealth Government to the invasion of Japanese Imperial forces in World War II to the return of the American GIs and the Americanization of the Philippines, to our independence from US colonization, and finally to today's globalization.

I feel that the topic I'd like to speak on this morning is not really about my businesses, my so-called "successes" but my perception, my freedom to express this perception on how we managed to lose our humanity to today's conflicts. So, I'd like to talk on the subject "The Promises We Made".

Still shackled

More than a hundred years ago, our forefathers stood together, in courage and sacrifice, to declare our country's independence. It came like the brilliant dawn ending a long night of struggle to end Spain's stranglehold on her colony. Filipinos rose up in joy and hope, anxious to end centuries of injustice, inequality and oppression.

But a hundred years later, the Filipino is still not free. One hundred years later, the chains of political, religious and class divisions continue to shackle the Filipino. One hundred years later, our archipelago has become island prisons of poverty separated from the prosperity seen so clearly in other lands. One hundred years later, the Filipino finds himself disadvantaged in his own home, denied protection of the law and forced into exile from his own land to find sustenance and livelihood.

We have had other so-called revolutions that others hoped would bring true emancipation for the Filipino. The upheaval of 1986 brought a moment of hope when the framers of the New Constitution made a new promise to every Filipino that became all our commitment when it was ratified. **It was a promissory note for justice, protection under the law and shared prosperity for all.**

There is no doubt that the Philippines has defaulted on this obligation. Worse than our inability to pay our onerous international debt, is how we have defaulted on our obligation to our people to give them the life they were promised.

But it is not the Promised Land, a land of milk and honey, the easy life, which we promised to deliver. We promised to make democracy work for them so that they may have **even only** the opportunity to work hard and persevere in their lives, to pull themselves out of the quicksand of poverty and climb up the way of knowledge and education.

It was a promise of enlightened leadership that would be sterling examples of integrity and competence.

It was a promise to give equal access to the laws, provide equal opportunities and an equitable justice system for all.

It was a promise to be pure and incorruptible. It was a promise to serve only the interest of the Filipino people and not for the benefit, privilege and advantage of the select few.

No bitterness

I was a poor little girl growing up in Leyte. Daughter of a poor shoemaker, I spent my days running around barefoot in the hot sun, delivering shoes, collecting payments, carrying drums of water heavier than me, doing household chores and all sorts of odd jobs. All this while I studied in our little town school.

I have no bitterness about my life and the struggles that followed. I only have joyful memories of how we persevered and worked together, all our earnings contributed to the family fund and dispensed according to the wisdom of my mother.

Despite all the hardship, our laughter was genuine, simple meals became feasts because they were shared, our sleep was deep and peaceful, our dreams filled with simple hopes and our prayers were populated by those we loved.

God has been so good to me, having blessed me with opportunities to work and study, which I would do into the wee horns of the morning while raising my family.

Combined with the perseverance and hard work ethic of my youth, my life advanced and progressed little by little, centavo by centavo, sweat upon tear. But never was riches my goal nor power my dream.

In all those years, I sought only the same genuine joy and laughter of my children and that they too would have dreams filled with simple hope.

And this, I believe, is the desire of the heart of every Filipino.

And as we share the same dream and are driven by the same love for our families, remember too that the fulfillment of our dreams is inextricably bound to the dreams of all our fellow Filipinos.

We are tied together; we cannot walk alone.

Call to heroism

We begin this walk by heeding the call to heroism and leadership that is stirring in your very souls as I speak.

Just as Moses, hidden away for many years in obscurity, emerges in courage and firmness of purpose, so must we arise and take on mantle of leadership to help the lost and discouraged.

It is worth dying for this great truth - our lives as Filipinos are but one life. You may be afraid, to lose your safety, your homes, your livelihoods, to be attacked and accused and therefore hide and live to be 80. But you will already have died.

For a man dies when he refuses to stand up for that which is right. A man dies when he refuses to stand up for justice. A man dies when he refuses to take a stand for that which is true.

We are the generation that knows and understands that our people must be set free from oppression.

To set them free, our democracy must work.

And to make it work, we must stand up for it, protect the institutions that give it life and resist the dark powers of greed and vested interests.

Never accept slavery

Never accept the chains of slavery to corruption and greed in exchange for life, no matter how sweet nor peaceful. Say no to corruption now. Demand integrity and honesty from all you deal and work with.

Work to uplift others by sharing what you have. For as much as you receive, give to others that they too may grow. This is the true balance of life that keeps the soul alive for nothing is left stagnant but instead you are filled with flowing, vibrant living waters.

Should Moses have told the children of Israel to live in slavery under the pharaoh? Should Christ have refused the Cross? Should the *katipuneros* have thrown down their guns and surrendered? Should our soldiers have not given up their lives in Bataan?

The martyrs of history were not fools. They knew that the road to freedom for Filipinos had to be bought at a price, a demanding price for all of us. Let us walk together in our common quest for a decent life, a virtuous life anchored on truth, justice, fair play, and love of our country always. Let us walk hand in hand as compatriots to our destiny.

XXXIII
Successful Succession Planning in Family-Owned Enterprises

Entrepinoy Volunteers Foundation, Inc. Business Clinic; December 4, 2001
NOTE: Prior to this talk, I and my son, David, attended an international conference on the same topic. I have integrated in this speech the insights, experiences and lessons shared by the participants in said conference who came from various countries.

Let me begin our session this morning with horror stories that strike the deepest fear in the hearts of family businesses.

Horror stories

Have you heard the news that Jerry died suddenly in the arms of his paramour and left his entire fortune in shambles? It was only then that his family learned about his
secret bank account and his immense debts. His family is completely devastated!

What about the grandson of Don Peping? He is practically a pauper as his grandfather's properties were foreclosed by the bank, chopped up and sold to strangers at giveaway values.

And then there is the ongoing legal squabble among the children of Rosario. Since her husband died in an accident, the family split into two camps who have been fighting for ten years to control the estate. Both sides have spent millions in legal fees and all they have to show for it are animosity, hatred, and deep emotional stress.

These are horror stories that occur in real life all too often. Poor financial planning results in severe losses in the transfer of resources to the next generation. Successors are often unprepared to manage the business into the next generation. Without a firm set of family values and rules, transition soon degenerates into courtroom drama.

Statistics on family businesses

We all know that the family is the foundation of both society and business, particularly in Asia. The goal to keep this family united and productive is not, an easy one, as the following statistics will show:

- In the United States a research conducted by R. Beckhand and W. Gib Dyer shows that 90% of the large businesses are family-owned which eventually became publicly listed companies.
- Family businesses did not survive one generation (or 25 years)
- Only three out of ten lasted until the second generation
- Similar conditions exist in Indonesia with few exceptions
- Among Chinese families, most businesses exist well up to the second generation and do not perform well by the third generation.

No succession plan, no business continuity plan

One major reason for these statistics is that family businesses seldom prepare a plan for succession and continuity of the business. There is very little conscious effort to prepare the next generation and no common understanding of how all members should work together.

For those of us in the family businesses and perhaps are now in the process of scanning the future of our families, the first step in establishing succession and continuity begins in the hearts and minds of our family members.

Laying the foundation

There are no shortcuts and there can be no hypocrisy when the founder commits to forming the hearts and minds of the successor generation'. Nor is there a time limit - it is never too early or too late to start laying the foundation of values, character building and corporate processes for family business members. They serve as a lighthouse, lasting guides to serve the generation to come. These are:

- Founders lead by example
- Nurture the successors
- Communicate the Succession Plan

And now, a more detailed discussion: **FOUNDERS LEAD BY EXAMPLE**

Live the Foundation Values

On a daily basis, children notice the priorities, lifestyle and ethical conduct of the founder. These reflect what **I** call **"Foundation Values."** True foundation values describe the **personal, moral and spiritual priorities** a person has and how they guide his life.

Decision-making and patterns of speech often reveal how committed the founder is to the foundation values espoused.

Even character traits such as equanimity in the face of trials, humor and compassion can be passed on through foundation values.

Communicate the values

The Foundation Values must be clear to you personally.

Share these values with the successors to help them understand the heritage that you are passing on to them and be consistent.

Your consistency in living your values and principles will greatly inspire the next generation's ability to commit to the family's business ideals.

NURTURE THE SUCCESSORS

The successors, your children, need to develop the character, attitudes and skills necessary to wholeheartedly adopt the foundation values you are trying to communicate. Remember that character and attitudes didn't just happen; they were formed by the passion and sacrifice of your life.

Some families opt to train their children themselves by bringing them in early into the business as summer apprentices and helpers.

Other families encourage their children to work in other companies first to gain experience as a professional and gain a different kind of discipline and business perspective.

Still others believe that the successors need to acquire certain exposure and knowledge through higher education.

Let me emphasize that the successors have free choices always which the founders should always respect and support.

I have four children who grew up in the same household and yet have emerged with different preferences and capabilities that have made themselves more distinct as the years go by.

I have always recognized this and have always done my best to nurture them according to their specific potentials and directions.

SUCCESSION PLANNING FACTORS

Succession is a conscious endeavor and must be pursued with a balance of measured caution and a sense of urgency. Completeness and swiftness requires everyone to participate and support the completion of the factors which include defining the following:

Family Values
- Love of God
- Love of country
- Love of family
- Love of neighbors and service communities '
- Fairplay, hardwork, professionalism and, above all, integrity
- A lifestyle reflecting humility, frugality, simplicity anchored on a spirit of sacrifice

Family Mission
- Our family's credo is an expression of our abiding faith in the goodness of man and respect for the qualities and traits that have strengthened and blessed us with some success.
- Our desire is to appreciate the source of our blessings and to share with all present and future members of our family the recognition and gratitude of the foundation which we build and will continue to grow;
- We honor the values built on the family foundation, which we hope to pass on to future generations as guideposts in our work and relationship.
- Our family members are of diverse talent and strength. We fully respect this diversity. Despite our differences, we commit to each other support, understanding and love, always. No dispute can tear our family bond. We aim to succeed under an environment of harmony so as to serve our society better.
- Our family's mission is to give leadership and good stewardship for the family business' total organization knowing that only through this can we provide opportunities for growth and prosperity four our family's future generations.
- We can achieve this by lending full support to the management of the family organization in their efforts to accomplish our family mission and objectives and educating future generations about the history and values of the family.

Terms and tips to consider
- The succession of the leadership in the family business is limited to the legitimate and blood-related family members. The seats could never be assigned to an outsider, which include spouses.
- The shares of the family members cannot be sold to an outsider. Corresponding legal documents will be drawn in order to safeguard the continuity of succession within the family.
- The family shall have full control of the finances and over-all operations of the business. The professional managers will be tasked to manage the day-to-day operations, subject to the control and

supervision of the family member-representatives. They are expected to make full reporting and accounting to the Managing Head and representatives.

- In order to face the very challenging responsibilities that go with their positions, future representatives and successors will be chosen based on educational attainment, moral character, capability, competence and leadership qualities to influence unity and good relationship among family members.
- While the family upholds high regard for good quality education, future representatives and successors must also possess emotional maturity.

Rules for settling conflicts

- Know that conflicts are destructive
- Imbibe family values in order to avoid conflicts
- If conflicts occur, it must never be on the issue of money but rather on principle
- Listen intently to one another with deep courtesy
- Get your facts crystal clear before conflict arises
- Always get all sides of the issue
- Seek understanding and wisdom
- Pray to the Lord; seek His guidance and light

Family pledge to management

- The family goal is to effect smooth transition of the business from one generation to another. This can be done by perpetuating the family values. Every generation pledges to work hard, support and trust the managing family head.
- The family pledges to meet regularly and communicate matters to the Board of Directors through the managing head of the family.
- The family pledges to fully support all the decisions, actions and plans that are approved by the Board
- The family pledges to respect nonfamily managers and to provide an environment wherein they are given the opportunity to work, grow and excel in their jobs.
- The family pledges to practice responsible ownership of the business, address issues within the walls of their meetings and speak to the Board with a single voice.

Once a decision has been made, it must be folly supported by all.

- The family pledges that its members exercise open-mindedness and sound judgment? in all their actuations to ensure fairness, transparency and noble benefits.

Simple values

My values and mission were simple:

- To give my best in every opportunity given to me by God; my best means to strive hard to always act with integrity, respect and decency
- To   promote family love and trust
- To   be a good example of an industrious and creative person
- To   be humble and frugal
- To   do work for the benefit of family and community
- To   appreciate and preserve nature and its abundance
- To encourage learning
- To   enjoy life with humor, laughter, compassion and accompanying challenges
- To   share benefits with all stake holders
- To   create a family business that adds value to the community and country through growth, creating wealth, adding resources and generation of jobs.

Family ownership management

Good assets are God's blessings, which are gained through hard work, fair play and decency.

These have to be safeguarded for the good of the family and all intertwined sectors of the family businesses (employees, shareholders, community and country).

Ownership structure is clearly delineated to ensure success in continuity. Stewardship should be in capable and responsible hands.

Organization should be carefully established to achieve the best results in running the business smoothly and ensuring growth and continuity.

Succession and continuity

Beyond the formal structures which must be established for future generations of the business, values and their impact on the society must be taught, trained and lived as a code of behavior at an early stage of the lives of the successors.

All roads lead to God

To be good is not enough. It must be encompassing to acknowledge and to thank and always dedicate the good for the glory of God from whom all things emanate.

XXXIV
A Legacy Remembered

Cocktail Reception of Sony Philippines, Inc.; Dusit Hotel Makati; March 21, 2002

My mother was a hardworking and disciplined woman. She lived simply, worked long and hard without complaint and concentrated on her priorities. She strictly imposed that disciplined life on us, her children.

But for all that we went through, I cannot think of someone who has molded my life and influences it so strongly up to now than my mother.

Listen to the words of American author Hope Edelman as speaks of a similar experience of her mother: "I am fooling only myself when I say my mother exists now only in the photograph on my bulletin board or in the outline of my hand or in the armful of memories I still hold tight. She lives on in everything I do. Her presence influenced who I was, and her absence influences who I am. Our lives are shaped as much by those who leave us as they are by those who stay. Loss is our legacy. Insight is our gift. Memory is our guide."

As one of the more senior people in this room, I have the distinct advantage of having experienced the legacy of courage, sacrifice and love of a generation before. Not knowing who we were, generations before us struggled, suffered and in many cases died so that we might have hope for our future.

A strong people and a healthy society remember and honor the people who built their history. A doomed nation is one whose people only think of today with no thought of the path traveled by their ancestors.

I bid a warm welcome to. our new friend Mr. Takashi Umeyama and an equally 'warm send-off to Mr. Kenji Sakai.

I do so remembering that we too are the generation carrying on the work of those before us for the sake of those to some after us.

Let us take this moment as an opportunity to remember all the men and women, those present and those in our past, who helped develop us and build our business with us. I say this with a certain amount of emotion because in my life, family and business has always been inexorably intertwined.

Sony would never have attained market leadership in the Philippines if not for the 100% passion of the Solid people who pledged their lives in its pursuit.

Perhaps in that sense, ultimately, we are all really just family - working together and helping each other to achieve the best we can so that our children and children's children may know what it is like to hope for a better future.

Perhaps real progress and peace begins with this realization.

Thank you and good evening to you all.

XXXV
Get Connected

Aiwa Dealer Product Launching Dusit Hotel Nikko; September 6, 2002

72 years ago, a girl-child was born to a poor, hard-working, honest and decent woman. She grew up bereft of all material things. A basic necessity like water was not available. Water had to be bought and brought home from a town market half a kilometer away.

The child grew up in an environment of peace until her life was shattered by the fiery second World War that devastated her country and impoverished her family even more. Struggling through the war days and the consequent liberation of her town by a general called Mac Arthur with a pipe in his mouth.

This child had dreams, she dreamt of being a teacher, then a doctor, and even a general, and finally, there were no more dreams but simply a contentment and peace, joy and acceptance: of whatever comes from God.

Connected to God

I am the girl-child from Tacloban. I learned my life's lessons from my mother. I did not look up at great world heroes to emulate. It was enough to have my mother as a role model.

Mother was a widow at barely 30 years old and had to nurture, cherish and bring up six children ranging in age from one to nine years. I was the second to the last.

Humming and singing

My best memory of my mother was that of a kind person who was always humming and singing whenever she's cooking, washing, ironing, sewing - doing all works of being both a mother and father.

I remember asking her why she was always humming and singing and her answer was simple: "I hum and sing because I'm happy to be alive."

I celebrate my life by thanking God for His gifts — life, sky with sunlight at day and moon and stars at night, earth with plants, trees, flowers, rivers, lakes - because all are teeming with life; children are all normal and well; co-workers helping one another; friends to love; a country at peace and being governed well. And most of all, a God I can talk to everyday.

My mother was not religious. She was at work every day. She had no maid. She did every household chore in addition to working in her store. But she never stopped humming and singing. She was totally connected to God by the way she lived her humble life. Every hum and song was a prayer thanking God for His gifts.

A wonderful connection

It was a great and wonderful connection. But this connection was immersed within a spirit of enthusiasm, sacrifice, perseverance, loyalty, humility, commitment, courage and decency.

No matter how difficult and challenging the task may be, the "Connection" with the Lord was the one and only reason that empowered her and this empowerment she bequeathed to me. I thank her for this lifelong lesson.

Today, I am old, somewhat retired, but still lively, happy and content that this connection with the Lord and faith and trust in Him were all the ANSWER to a good life. The secret is simple: "Get connected to our Lord." He wants us to do well in everything we do in our relationship with people, be it at home, at work or at play. But this is not enough. Doing well is not enough if you do not do good, too.

One company, two brands

Our occasion today is the launch of the new products of Aiwa. You know very well that Aiwa is now 100% owned by Sony.

The new challenge to Sony is to succeed in its business under One Company with Two Brands. The Sony technology is now in all Aiwa products. We have the challenge of promoting all these new products, which are now designed, produced and marketed by the one and ihe same company of Sony Corporation.

We have a job to do. Let's do this job well and most of all, do good in the process.

Doing good means our works must be totally connected to the Lord. Our works must be performed with the spirit of God, that it be done with His Quality of Love as the essence of our living. God's love means to do our task well - with truth and excellence, and most of all, to do our task for God, for the glory of our Lord.

Let us offer and dedicate our lives to Him. Let us lift our hearts and minds to God and tell Him our aspiration:

"Father, in Jesus' name, with the Holy Spirit, we ask for your Connection with us in all our works. We need this Connection because this world offers much temptation that may detract us from doing good. Please give us the strength and courage to stay firm on our journey in doing well and good on this earth and keep our eyes focused on the Connectivity with You always."

XXXVI
How Women Succeed in Business

Acceptance of "[Outstanding Woman in Business" Award 5th Anniversary of the Filipino-Chinese Federation of Business and Professional Women of the Philippines Wack-Wack Golf & Country Club, Mandaluyong City; March 26, 2004

I am honestly always surprised to be honored and especially by this august gathering of accomplished business and professional women. Perhaps it is because for the last seven decades and five years, it never occurred to me that my struggles and beliefs would earn me anything more than what was enough for my daily needs.

I am very flattered to know that you have found this lady to have something in her life worth emulating despite my obvious disparity in age with some of you. Perhaps it is because we are looking for something more essential that transcends age and even generations and translates into all languages and cultures. You and I will determine if such an enduring treasure is to be found as we speak tonight.

Problems in governance, turbulent conditions and demanding markets

So, in these difficult and uncertain times, when we face the daunting challenges posed by globalization and international competition; when we cope with the gross inefficiencies and unparalleled corruption in national and local governance; when our society seems to crumbling under the weight of rampant crime and dissipating moral values, what does this lady before you have to offer?

Many years ago there was a scrawny barefoot little girl who sold tomatoes in the village market and ran around barefoot helping the struggling family business. Against all odds, she grew up to be involved with major manufacturing businesses with brands such as Sony, Samsung, Aiwa, and Sanyo. She grew up to spearhead the marketing of car brands such as KIA and BMW. She was involved in the development of industrial estates, pioneering prawn farming and export and challenging entrenched monopolies in the electronics, car, and cable industry.

That little girl faced her own set of challenges of growing up amidst the rubble of a postwar economy, with no resources and living basically a hand-to-mouth existence. She faced long hours of diligent work and study to get her through her education. She. faced stiff business competition and challenged government red tape to build her businesses while raising her family. What could she possibly have in her that saw her through all those years up to this evening here in front of you?

Let me tell you what it was: **She understood and shared the values of her mother.**

Woman's Critical Role - Nurturing Values

My mother was a strong-willed woman who faced the challenges' of life squarely in the face with an unyielding commitment to her principles that would not wane up to her dying day. And with the same fierce determination, she sought to instill the same in all her children. So, not only did I share the values of my mother but also so did my brothers and sisters. **We all understood and shared the same values.** No matter what our differences were in personality, character or dreams, all these differences were put aside and we were totally united under the leadership of my mother that was defined by the rules of her household. **Unity was more important** for the good of the family. Personal preferences were put aside in favor of obedience knowing that the greater good of the family was being served. Whatever sibling conflicts we may have had, they too had to be set aside when final decisions were made.

Household chores, helping with the business, doing schoolwork, sharing our personal income with the family and career choices were **all guided by her principles and rules, whether or not she was around.**

And her post-performance audit of our family duties was excellent as evidenced by her corrective actions often administered to my little bottom. **She always let us clearly know when we didn't live up to her values and rules.** No matter how you look at it, my mother, the woman of the house, had the special role of the nurturer of value system of our family - its backbone and reason for survival.

Shared values - essential to corporate survival

Now I am not saying that my mother was saintly, meek and mild. Quite the contrary, she was strong-willed and very stubborn about many things. On many occasions, there may have been a better way to do things, but once the decision was made, we all fell in line and did what we had to do for the family.

In those difficult days, we hardly had the luxury to spend days debating on the merits of every option. Urgency and survival rode on the timeliness of our actions. Our wholehearted support as a family helped us to survive when decisions were less than perfect and results were even less appealing.

Just as my family survived and later flourished on a unity based on shared values, so does any other corporate body. There is no company, no matter how many geniuses there are on the board that will not make mistakes or run into trouble. In those times, the bpard and officers need an external reference point, a guiding star that will guide them through turbulent times when vision is often clouded by personal emotions or conflicting ideas. Shared Values enables them to sort out ideas, emotions and agenda in a manner that everyone can support.

A woman's proactive nurturing

For some reason of divine purpose, a woman seems to be genetically more capable of nurturing values in an organization, whether in a family or a business. Perhaps it is because we are gifted with a nurturing spirit, which draws people together. Because we are so gifted, we must not be reticent about what we must do. Instead we must proactively and aggressively nurture shared values in our families and our organization.

Let me share with you three simple guidelines that I have learned:

1. **Communicate consistently and clearly**

Communicating values is not an oratorical contest. It is a relationship. It starts with clarity regarding what values you have or wish to promote. And then this is communicated consistently by both words and actions to express how these values are lived within the organization. It must be expressed again and again and then some more. Studies show that a human being must hear something at least three times before they begin to absorb it. All this does not happen by accident so we must somehow create formal or informal activities where these values are expressed and learned.

2. **Shared values must build unity**

There are many good values, morals and beliefs but too many to integrate and many times a source of conflict in themselves. Too many wars have been fought in the name of morality or religion. I come here not to promote specific values but encourage you to examine your own values and select a few that all in your organization can rally around and find unity in them.

3.   **Universal commitment**

Shared values don't mean anything unless everyone, and I mean everyone, commits to live by them. You can debate all you want in the boardroom but when you step outside, the values kick in and you are just one united force. It's the only way to survive in these difficult days. If you step out of line, it's made clear to you that you have to get back in line. This is especially true for family businesses that hire professionals. It must be made clear that the family has certain values and they either imbibe the values as their own or leave. You can't work as a team if you aren't sure about your teammates. Then you know that no matter where or what the situation is, you know how each member of the team will act.

There is much that I would have wanted to share with you regarding the values that worked for me all these years but I wanted to spend tonight first to explain why determining and instilling such values are so important in the first place. From selling tomatoes to building businesses or just nurturing your family, you women have the special calling to proactively establish shared values as the backbone of our families, our businesses and hopefully one day, our society.

Be strong and courageous as you do it and never be discouraged. For we do this not just for ourselves but so that our children's children may inherit from us families, businesses and a society committed to and united by values that are timeless, universal and bring peace and unity.

Good night and thank you.

XXXVII
There are No Barriers to Your Dreams Except Yourself

Career Guidance Symposium organized by MAPUA Institute of Technology and Rotary Club of Intramuros; MAPUA, Manila, October 20, 2004.

I am excited to stand before you today because I have the opportunity to begin by honoring a graduate from Mapua much like yourselves but from a different generation.

He graduated from the College of Electrical Engineering.

Subsequently, he earned a masters degree in mathematics and statistics. He went on to earn another masters degree in actuarial science from the University of Michigan and fell short of his Doctorate degree by three months, mainly due to the lack of scholarship funds.

Patriot

Even so, he was offered a senior position in the United Nations - which he turned down. He was offered a high-paying job in a Hong Kong based company - he turned it down too. You see, he was a government scholar and believed that it was his duty to serve his country, to return to help the men and women who supported him. **He would not let down those who believed in him.**

And return home he did. Without thought of his own personal gain, he worked tirelessly to design and build the Actuarial Science system of our country's, social security system, which is still being used today.

He has authored two books in this field, *"Rational Polynomial Equations"'* and *"Sen System of Arithmetic",* in the hope that he would be able to share, his expertise and learning with as many Filipinos as he could. **Knowledge, for him, was something to be shared, not exploited.**

He could have been the one delivering this address today. He lived his life in single-minded pursuit of excellence in his craft. His pursuit was guided by the **character and beliefs that he valued more than material wealth or recognition.**

He is my brother, Mr. Pedro Sen.

Unfortunately; his battle with Parkinson's disease makes it difficult for him to speak or travel. But his heart remains alive with the desire to use his knowledge to touch other people's lives.

Working student

My life has not been marked with the same academic excellence as Pedro's, but the same family values and character drove me to excel at what I did. I was a working student most of my life, balancing my time between studying and working to help my family, and later, to raise my children. Many of the schools where I earned my degrees no longer exist - perhaps a sign of how humble my origins were that I had to pursue my education where I could. But despite my constant lack of time and shortage of money, I managed to earn my degree in education and later in law.

I owe my law degree to the University of the East which also conferred on me an honorary doctorate in humanities, anchored on my 50 years of entrepreneurship which employed more than 10,000

Filipinos and uplifted the lives of their families.

I believe the achievement of your dreams is only limited by your own willingness to strive and sacrifice for it. It was Rudyard Kipling who said, "Humble because of knowledge, mighty by sacrifice." While you should not expect anyone to hand you anything on a silver platter, no difficulty should stop you from pursuing self-improvement and education.

There are no shortcuts to fulfilling of your dreams. It comes from a lifetime of discovering, building and sharing of the strengths and talents that lie within you. Trials and obstacles, though painful, will cut away what is unimportant and reveal what is essential and lasting.

Let me share with you some of the values and character traits that I have discovered that have served me in my journey through the years.

Perseverance

I was a barefoot little girl in the poor side of Tacloban, Leyte. My father was a shoemaker who struggled to make ends meet. That meant that all his children, including myself, had to do their share.

Every day, I carried a thick bamboo stick over my shoulder with two huge kerosene cans filled with water hanging on both ends. I would joke with my mother many years later that I should have been taller if not for carrying those water cans.

But my most important duty was to collect payments from customers who bought our shoes and slippers. It was our more affluent customers who bought on credit while bur neighbors and friends normally paid in cash.

It was my job to walk to their large houses and high gates to collect payment. Every day it would be the same. They would scold me for coming too early in the morning. Then they would scold me for disturbing their lunch. Then they said it was bad luck to pay at sundown.

I returned to their house the next day. And the next several days again until I finally received payment. Despite how I was treated, I harbored no personal ill will or even frustration. I was just focused on getting my job done. **It was there that I learned the power of perseverance.**

Perseverance demands that you stay focused on your purpose despite delays, obstacles and even emotions. They will all pass away as you pursue your goal. In my many years in business, the character trait of perseverance has served me best in my dealings with international business and government.

Faith in the Filipino

It saddens me that so many of our countrymen feel that the only path to progress is finding a job abroad. **"Anywhere but the Philippines"** seems to be the cry of our youth.

Our generation has failed because we have not had faith in the Filipino. We have started to believe that anything Filipino is corrupt, disorganized and highly politicized and will lead to nothing.

But I tell you today that the Filipino is proud and honorable, capable of doing great things if we, Filipinos ourselves, believe in Filipinos.

A classic example is our manufacturing experience with Sony electronics.

In 1978, our factories were manufacturing Sony televisions under the supervision of Japanese engineers.

Those engineers, while helpful, were very expensive to our operations and kept the Filipino engineers from growing into management positions.

I believed that we could prosper faster if the Japanese engineers were sent home and Filipinos were allowed to take their place.

I decided to make a trip to Tokyo to visit Dr. Yoshida, the number three man of Sony at that time to make that request.

My colleagues and family were all against the idea, as they felt-it would risk our whole business at the hands of "local engineers".

But I stuck to my principle to have Faith in the Filipino and went off on my mission.

In our meeting in Tokyo, Dr. Yoshida listened quietly and never commented as I presented my impassioned plea.

I asked him to return a sense of honor back to the Filipino engineers in our factory and allow them to operate the factory on their own.

I was not sure of what he thought as he responded with only a polite nod of the head.

But a few months later, I received the news that Dr. Yoshida had placed Philippine operations under his direct supervision and eventually allowed Filipino engineers to manage without Sony representatives.

We were touched by the faith that Dr. Yoshida had given the Filipino engineers and we were determined to do our best to honor his faith in us.

Please remember that we were the only Sony manufacturing plant in the world to operate without a Japanese engineer present in the plant so we knew that Dr. Yoshida was also taking a risk in supporting us.

The result was that both our morale and productivity went up ahd our factory became a model for the region. Put your **faith in the Filipino** and he will rise to the occasion!

Giving the best

I will end my talk by returning to the story of my brother.

The reason that he made such an impact in his field of actuarial science was that he focused on using his skills and knowledge to improve other people's lives. He was driven by the desire to seek **constant improvement in service first.** He was focused on raising others above their ordinary lives and discover a higher calling of excellence. **He wanted to give his best and draw out the best from others.**

Satisfaction and profit were simply byproducts of a job well done.

Every business I ever went into had to have the capacity to uplift the minds and souls of my countrymen, not just daily physical needs.

I have always sought businesses that would uplift the **quality of being and not just the quality of living** of those I served. Carl Jung once said, **"the sole purpose of human existence is to kindle the light in the darkness of mere being."**

Our real challenge today is much more than the economy and the government. Our true challenge lies within our own hearts, holding on to our dreams and pursuing them.

There are no limits on your dreams except your willingness to pursue them with **perseverance,** to work together with others in common **Faith in the Filipino,** in order to **give the best** we can so that the quality of being of our fellow Filipinos will be uplifted.

Thank you very much and good day to you all!

XXXVIII
Be an Inspiring Generation

Keynote address before the ANVIL Business Club (now renamed Association of Young Filipino Chinese Entrepreneurs) composed of the young sons and daughters of Filipino-Chinese business leaders (the tycoons of many industries and businesses). Held in a Makati hotel sometime after 2000.

It is my privilege to speak before you today, a dynamic group of young Filipino- Chinese entrepreneurs who hold much promise, as you lead and inspire your colleagues and fellow entrepreneurs.

I have a simple message for you. Be an inspiring generation like the generations who came before you.

The only way to truly honor the past. is by your works of nobility and ingenuity, in the present and future, which will shine brightly and radiate excellence that reflect the culture and values of the Filipino.

All the young men and women I see in this room, young and successful Filipino- Chinese entrepreneurs, members of your Anvil Business Club, have one thing in common: You are the fortunate inheritors, the beneficiaries of your forebears who have worked under extreme sacrifices under harrowing times to attain their great fortunes.

Your forebears

They who took a leap a leap of faith from Mainland China and came to a strange new land called the Philippines during the Spanish, American, and Japanese occupations.

They came armed with nothing more than hard, work and passion to eke out a living in a strange country, against great adversities that were threatening, lonely, and despairing.

Just imagine how your forebears, who hardly spoke a word of the local language and English, had to struggle.

It was not easy, especially with the enactment of the Law of Exclusion against Chinese Immigrants, compounded with the bias and discrimination exhibited by both the foreign occupants and the local inhabitants.

Surely, your forebears must have gritted their teeth in humility to survive such a hard and unfriendly environment.

It was only through their instinct for survival and strength of character and endurance that they weathered the days and slowly turned such hostilities and challenges to a stronger and calmer inner trait and even managed to succeed. Such was their time of anxiety and chaos.

Survival mode

To survive and blend into those times, a special grit was required.

They may have practiced business skills that today would be unacceptable.

They slaved and suffered internally and physically. Many of them were murdered, massacred, and even burned in their homes.

Rules and regulations were cruelly set against them, despite the special skills they offered their adopted country as tailors, cooks, masons, tinsmiths, carpenters, engineers, and many other professions; skills which they gradually made part of the mainstream of daily Filipino life.

It would be many years and decades, however, before they would find their fortunes.

Their skills in business found their fortunes changed as the years rolled on. They lived frugal, humble, simple lives. Maybe, they didn't have to pay taxes, and if they did, surely barely exceeding the minimum.

But thanks to their sacrifices and accomplishments, you are today their pride. You are learned, brilliant, and have the best education to be proud of.

You can now afford to have strategic, long term plans, unlike your forebears who had more than they could handle just to ensure daily survival.

I call this to mind because from their years of survival and hard work, they managed to upgrade their status in society.

Many became pioneers of various industries, and rich. But in their richness, they exhibited humility and simplicity in their ways. Surely, a contrast to you today who are leaders in your chosen fields of endeavors, assisted by the inheritance from your forebears to live lives of grace, abundance, and special blessings.

The familiar saying "With great power comes great responsibility" is particularly apt for you. The great power and wealth bestowed on you through the immense sacrifices and toil of your parents and grandparents come with even greater responsibility.

Such as the responsibility to do business or practice your profession in the right way, to treat all parties fairly, to do business or trade in a fair and honest manner.

Concretely, this means, among others, paying the right taxes, getting the right licenses, permits, acquisitions, franchises, or concessions through legal and ethical processes, without compromising fundamental values. It also means regularization of employees who have duly qualified and passed their probationary period, instead of the infamous practice of five months labor contractualization to avoid compulsory regularization after six months.

Don't emulate survival measures

While I call on you to emulate the diligence, courage, perseverance, thrift, and hard work of your forebears, I also call on you not to emulate the survival measures, the unethical short cuts, compromises that redound to unfairness and dishonesty that, perhaps, some of them took during their difficult times or when rules and regulations were implemented wrongly.

You are now in positions to be great leaders in the urgent and glorious task of building a truly great, prosperous, and just Filipino nation. I pray you will live up to the task and the responsibility.

Thank you and please do not take offense at my propensity to be politically incorrect because of my candid talk. It is not my character to praise, flatter, or condescend when I feel that my late age and experiences will be good tools in influencing you to become better and nobler in your lives. From you and your experiences will flow ideas and great entrepreneurial accomplishments that will affect the lives of many who will be benefited by your inspiring life.

Emulate right values

I assure you: Emulating the right values, the character, the humility, and simplicity of your forebears will reap you rewards beyond your wildest imagination.

I thank you for your indulgence in listening to my talk which has been, perhaps, unlike the talks you are used to hearing from other speakers, far better talented and equipped, far more politically correct, than my humble person.

POSTSCRIPT
Of Sinners, Camels, and Pigs

This speech before ANVIL's young Filipino-Chinese entrepreneurs brings to mind other short talks I delivered on similar topics, such as the one before our employees and guests during the inauguration of our shrimp/prawn processing plant in Bacolod, sometime in the mid-eighties, shortly before the 1986 EDSA People Power Revolt which ousted the Marcos Dictatorship in a miraculously bloodless manner.

At that time, the political situation was highly unstable. The assassination of former Senator Benigno "Ninoy" Aquino on August 21, 1983, triggered countless rallies and massive capital flight.

To prevent total bankruptcy, the Marcos regime employed desperate measures to raise funds to avoid defaulting on its massive loans, as well as to sustain government operations and social services. Lack of funds for government programs would lead to more hardships for the citizenry, thus greater political turmoil.

One of those measures was the Central Bank bill called "Jobo bill," after the nickname of former Central Bank Governor Jose B. Fernandez who initiated it. The Jobo Bill offered an almost irresistible 45% interest rate to those who bought it.

Camels

In this context, I had the choice of buying 20 million pesos worth of Jobo bills instead of investing in a very risky prawn business venture. Through Jobo bills, I could double my P20 million in two years, risk-free, without having to go through the nightmarish process of building an infrastructure to process shrimps for export which would entail many years of development, with no assurance of success.

It was a period of great stress and hardship in Bacolod as they lost traditional markets for their once-vaunted sugar exports, a victim of changing market conditions. It was precisely in this tumultuous period that I decided to put up the prawn processing plant in Bacolod.

During the Holy Mass for the inauguration, the late Bacolod Bishbp Antonio Fortich shared the parable of Jesus on how it would be easier for a camel to pass through the eye of a needle than for a rich man to enter the Kingdom of Heaven.

I was taken aback by his homily. I felt uneasy, sensing that he was somehow alluding to me. In my short response to his talk, I said: "How timely, indeed, Monsignor, are your words of wisdom to caution the rich about the difficulty of entering God's kingdom even with their vast resources and money.

"But isn't it just as difficult to enter the Kingdom of Heaven ifa man lives a life of self-indulgence, abandoning his familial duties by engaging in drinking bouts and petty gambling, such as what many country folks practice?

"Surely he cannot be saved by merely being poor per se. He is as unworthy of heaven as the wealthy man who gains wealth through foul means such as bribery, conspiracy, and collusion with corrupt public officials who allow him to prosper by avoiding payment of duties and taxes to the government, who gains unlawful monies by behest loans, concessions bom out of corruption and monopolies to the detriment of the public.

"Surely the Lord God Almighty who is all just can wield the same sword against poor and rich alike who defile His commandments. I say Amen to your words of wisdom, Monsignor, because I believe with all my heart, mind, and soul that honest work will also earn the Lord s smile. I pray the good Father in Heaven will shine to all of us here today to do work honestly and to serve our neighbors faithfully.

"My P20 million to start this pioneer processing plant in Bacolod will do honor to Him by harnessing the power, talent, and love of our countrymen to serve both our nation and our Lord. We will pay fair wages and pay taxes due to government, too."

The people in attendance clapped their hands loudly in glee.

Pigs

At about this period my friend, David Tan, a son of my compadre Anthony, came to me almost crying that his pigs at his piggery farm called Bonanza in Laguna were hungry and weak, about to die of starvation, because he had ran out of working capital to buy feed.

Because of the 45% interest offered by Jobo bills, banks were also charging very high interest for their loans. Like virtually all entrepreneurs, he simply could not afford to borrow from banks at 45% interest. It was like picking a rock to pound on his head. '

In the meantime, many of his piglets were dying while he was scouting for money to buy feeds. He was facing a blank wall. No one, no one would give him the money to buy the feeds. I asked him how much he needed. He said PI 5 million will tide him over, at least to save the remaining pigs. I gave him the money and told him not to worry about the interest. Just save your pigs first. By God's grace, the amount sufficed and he saved his farm. He paid me back the loan after the crisis.

Many years later, when I asked him to help me look for a small farm to raise horses, he did me the favor of finding my present small farm in Calamba, Laguna which is an oasis of peace, prayer, and pleasure to all who stay in the farm. Thank you, David Tan. You are a good man and Jesus loves you very much.

These three stories are somehow interconnected because they all took place at the same time when the Jobo bill was the bitter medicine the government imposed on us. Also, in all those instances, money and integrity were the fundamental issues.

I was given the courage to speak before the young entrepreneurs of ANVIL and the people gathered At my Bacolod Plant inauguration to trust God and not to do "shortcut" business and yes, pay due taxes to government. "Give to God what is God's and to Caesar what is Caesar's." This is a hard topic but I find strength to say my piece when called for. Praise the Lord!

XXXIX
UNFAIR TRADE, THEN AND NOW

Synthesis of highlights from Welcome Address to journalists and Inspirational Talk before MyPhone employees; January 2013

In my six decades of entrepreneurship, my greatest joy has always been in speaking out and seeking just resolution of certain unfair deals that Filipinos have had to endure.

I'd like to share with you two memorable events that brought to fore my deep love and respect for Filipino pride and talent.

Whenever I see these violated for the narrow self-interest of a few, whether from foreigners or Filipinos, I always find my voice to loudly protest the wrong and misdeed even at the expense of my person being ostracized, shamed and humiliated. I do not mind this unkind cut to me but I do mind whenever inequity and unfair practices are imposed on the Filipino and our country.

I live by what is right and just, both personally and professionally.
"Excuse me, Mr. President"

Sometime in 1976 or 1977, a few years after he declared Martial Law on September 21, 1972, President Ferdinand Edralin Marcos invited over a hundred business executives to a dialogue in Malacanang Palace.

Security was very tight. In effect, we had to go through three checkpoints. First, at the gate, where our identities were checked against an official list of invited guests. Second, at the ground lobby where we were given guest ID cards and subjected to a thorough security check to ensure we were not carrying deadly weapons or banned items (cameras, tape recorders, etc.). The third and final check was at the entrance to Maharlika Hall, located on the second floor,where the dialogue w;ould be held.

This was the first formal meeting between Marcos and the business sector during Martial Law. Apparently, he wanted to feel the pulse of business, get a sense of how business people perceived martial rule. He wanted to elicit directly from the business leaders what martial rule had contributed to their business. Most of all, it seemed he wanted to get AFFIRMATION that Martial Law was good for business.

He would call Mr. So-and-so and ask "How is your business doing now?" Then he would smile pleasantly when a top honcho would say something like "Mr. President, my business sector is doing very fine. The workers are Working hard and the output is much better than before Martial Law," etc., etc.

During Martial Law, strikes were banned and so, to a certain extent, there was truth to the claim of "industrial peace." In the same manner, all forms of dissent were banned, such as rallies and a free press. This led many critics of the Marcos Dictatorship to say that, indeed, Martial Law brought peace to the Philippines - the peace of the graveyard. Certainly not peace based on truth, authentic democracy, justice, and shared prosperity.

Throughout the meeting, my colleagues gave very positive remarks about the Marcos Administration which greatly pleased the President.

As the meeting was about to end and the President was already half-out of his seat, I rushed to a microphone and said, "Excuse me, Mr. President, I will be remiss in my duty if I do not bring to your attention a very serious matter in the export of shrimp and other seafood items."

The conference moderator was aghast at my temerity and made frantic gestures for me to go back to my seat. However, I had already gotten the President's attention. He sat down again and said, "Let the lady speak."

I forgot to mention my name, but I blurted out, "The export of shrimp is just a new business and already it is burdened by a 4% tax on the FOB value, which is the value of goods excluding carriage, insurance and freight. This tax is onerous, unfair and without justification other than simply for revenue purpose. Yet its objective will not get the desired revenue because the industry is dying and there will be no taxes at all to collect. This export of shrimp is a new growing business and needs to be supported, not taxed. We are the ONLY country in the world which imposes a 4% tax on total export value on shrimp and prawns. Other countries even give special support like financing, efficient infrastructure and tax incentives. The shrimp is 100% indigenous product and does not require any imported part to be incorporated."

The President was taken aback at my forthrightness but calmly asked me three questions: The amount of the tax, the people affected, and how it compared with other Asian countries. I answered all three questions satisfactorily and justified the immediate removal of said tax because it was unjust, onerous, without rhyme nor reason for its existence.

Where did I find the courage to confront President Marcos despite his awesome martial law powers? At that time, he was at the peak of his dictatorial rule. Virtually no one dared to contradict him openly for fear of possible consequences.

I was not cowed into meekness, though, because I truly believed this 4% export tax was without basis and would ruin a good, promising business, affecting countryside people like fishermen, processors, transport workers, and many others. There was no hesitation in my voice. It was the voice of a Filipino who understood the evil consequences of the 4% tax on our economy and people. I love our Filipino people and our beautiful country. There is strength and sincerity in my voice to uplift ourselves from poverty. Every business counts. Every Filipino counts.

The end to this drama was the dramatic response of the President. On the spot he ordered the removal of the 4% export tax on shrimp and directed Commissioner Farolan and Minister Villafuerte to implement his order at once.

I was both relieved and astonished at his instant and decisive action on my request. This could only happen under a Martial Law environment.

I must say, though, that despite the speed of his decision and action, I would still prefer the democratic process, wherein policies are subjected to mature and intelligent deliberation by responsible legislators. Through such a process, it is likely that wrong policies like the 4% export tax would have been avoided, in the first place.

There is an important caveat, though. The democratic process will work best only when we have leaders and legislators who have great integrity, patriotism, and intellect. Leaders in the mold of Filipino statesmen such as Jose, W. Diokno, Claro M. Recto, Lorenzo Tanada, Jose Laurel, Sr. and his son, Speaker Jose Laurel, Jr. and many others. Unfortunately, these great men are no longer with us.

Another interesting aspect to this incident was that prior to the dialogue with the President, our Shrimp Association was consulting a law firm to lobby for us for the removal of the 4% tax. We could not agree on the legal fee because the Association could not afford it.

But by God's will, in a timely moment, President Marcos immediately removed the tax upon my personal request and ex-planation. Indeed, the Lord works miracles in His own time. This was one such time. A living example that life or business can take sudden, miraculous, happy endings.

Another lesson I learned in life: "Be truthful, brave, and speak up when you feel strongly about the righteousness of your cause. Keep faith in your passion for any pursuit of the IDEAL. The reward is always sweet and fulfilling."

Persona non grata

My other example happened in 1986, the first year of the EDSAI uprising.

The bloodless coup had just ended. President Cory Aquino invited the Keidan- ren Top Executives of Japan to come to the Philippines and invest. Out of admiration for our new President Cory Aquino, the Keidanren immediately came (over 100 top Japanese CEOs and

COOs).

A conference at the PICC was convened with four speakers from each side.

The Japanese side had four CEOs as speakers who spoke heartily congratulating our victorious EDSA 1 and committing support for the Aquino government. The four Filipino speakers responded. I was the only female speaker among the four speakers.

Sensing this as a great opportunity to catch the attention of the mighty Keidanren, the foremost economic advisory body to the Japanese government, I researched and wrote my speech with candidness.

It was my hour and a chance to get across to the mighty Keidanren some issues needing immediate attention for mutual benefits and respect.

I was emboldened to ask the Keidanren to help address certain kinks in our trade relations and hoped for their kind understanding and to address unfairness such as:

1) Investment should be geared towards

development and sustainable growth in industries, not merely screw-type operation;

2) Respect Filipino executives by recognizing their talents and giving them equitable salaries;

3) Help curb illegal overshipment/smuggling of logs to Japan (then our biggest importer of logs). Deforestation has done not just great damage to our environment; it has also taken thousands of Filipino lives due to flooding.

I was, of course, met with shock and awe from some of the participants, both Filipino and Japanese.

I didn't falter. I kept focused on my mission to get the Golden Opportunity to address long outstanding irritants whether in business or in social network. The result was a plus factor for us Filipinos. Reforms were instituted in the matter of visas (upon certain recommendations I voiced out).

The President of Phillips, a Dutch CEO, told me that he was touched by my speech and repatriated all his expats, leaving him alone in the Philippines - clear proof of how deeply he realized the true value of Filipino talent.

All these radical changes would never have happened had I not boldly and respectfully brought them to the attention of the Keidanren.

A million thanks to the beautiful and righteous Keidanren for hearing and resolving the irritants of our relationship.

Without the Keidanren, we would never have enjoyed the changes made in both our business and personal relationships.

Smuggling of cell phones?

From the eighties to mid-2000, the mobile phone industry was dominated by foreign brands. There was a total absence of Filipino brands. MyPhone, a 100% Filipino brand and owned 100% by Filipinos came into our market only in the year 2007.

This new breed of Filipinos dared to challenge the foreign brands and decided to change the game that once existed only for foreign brands. Changing the game means being innovative and competitive by giving a truly inclusive quality cell phone for all walks of life. The poor deserve a good quality cell phone with features truly Filipino in the heart of the phone that embraces our culture of religion, laughter, and enjoyment of our Filipino music, riddles, sayings of the old embedded in the software of the phone at very competitive prices, well within the reach of our numerous "masa."

Solid's MyPhone has put into the hands of millions of our people high quality mobile phones, covered by full warranty and after-sales service - from cities to the small villages in the provinces. It has brought forth thousands of SMEs whose lives have been changed by servicing all their customers with phones at par with foreign brands. But most of all, every unit of MyPhone is fully tax-paid. Every unit has the approval of the National Telecommunications Commission (NTC) as to the quantity applied for.

At this point, allow me to quote from the column HIDDEN AGENDA by Mary Ann LI. Reyes published in the Philippine Star last October 26,2011. It goes: *"Sad to say, some foreign brands of mobile phones have been misdeclaring their actual imports, not only to avoid paying such fees to the NTC but also the proper customs duties and taxes.*

"Based on data obtained from the NTC by the complainants, about 1.99 million handsets have been imported and covered by import permits for the period January to May 2011. At an average of 397,690 handsets per month, this figure is grossly understated since independent research data show that the Philippine market averages 600,000 units per month.

"Compared to MyPhone s importation of 769,616 handsets which makes it the number one importer of NTC registered phones, Nokia and Cherry Mobile phones covered by NTC permits to import total only 37,551 and 8,920, respectively, which is absurd, considering that

Nokia claims to be number one in the Philippines and Cherry Mobile's sales volume as per GFK data average 300,000per month.

"Imported handsets covered by NTC permits of Sony Ericsson and Apple amount to 686 and 17, respectively. To think that Globe Telecom is targeting to sell 200,000 IPhones on the average per month.

"Samsung, based on the NTC data, imported 888,000 units, BlackBerry 59,880, LG 59,808, HTC 1,1770, Motorola six units.

"Government is losing huge amounts of money from this underdeclaration. Assuming that the underdeclaration is around 202,310per month, at an average ofP3,000 price per phone, that would be P606.9 million in potential revenues. VAT collections alone would amount to P72.8 million.

"BIR Commissioner Kim Henares and Customs Commissioner Ruffy Biazon have already been informed of the glaring discrepancies. They just have to compare the number of imported cellphones covered by NTC permits to import and correlate the data with those that BIR and BOC have." (end of quote)

If, as the article notes, government is losing around P73 MILLION PESOS PER MONTH in uncollected VAT (Value Added Tax) because of the alleged smuggling of cell phones, can you imagine how much government has lost for the past 20 years? This implies almost a billion pesos of unpaid VAT per year! Can you imagine how many school buildings, hospitals, roads, bridges, etc., we could have built with 20 billion pesos? Can you imagine how many life-saving medicines could have been purchased with 20 billion pesos?

As required by law under NTC Circular 300, all importation of phones should be approved by NTC as to its quantity. Such a glaring discrepancy between actual units sold and the units approved by NTC could only prove that there is much technical or outright smuggling of foreign brand phones in order to evade payment of taxes.

Is this fair? Of course not. MyPhone has only been in the market for five years and it has its import application in the correct number and every unit is fully tax- paid. We have had to suffer huge expenses in development, creating Filipino inputs for our software, hiring hundreds of employees, and paying every unit with its corresponding tax.

Isn't this alleged practice of foreign brands shortchanging the public and the government of its mandated tax a felony? If it is, where are the remedial actions of the agencies concerned, such as Customs,

BIR and NTC? Has anything changed? Where is the *"Daang Matuwid"* (Righteous Path)?

Numerous complaints have been filed by adversely affected parties with these agencies. So far, no action. This sounds like a *deja vu* of my Tuner Fiasco over 25 years ago wherein the joint venture companies (foreigners) refused to buy a single unit of tuner from my accredited pioneer status Filipino company and yet, somehow, still managed to sell their locally manufactured TV without any documented tuner import.

A truly mysterious phenomenon, since all their TV sets had tuners and there was no other legitimate local producer of tuners except my company. Since they didn't buy from me, where did they get their tuners? I guess if Sherlock Holmes could still be consulted, most likely he would say: "Elementary, my dear Elena. They smuggled their tuners!"

Now, in the case of alleged cell phone smuggling, if I could only talk to Sherlock Holmes, I would tell him: "This case is less than elementary, my dear Sherlock. All that government has to do is COMPARE the actual sales figures of cell phone brands in the Philippines with their official applications for NTC permits, their official importation records at Customs, and their official tax payments to BIR."

To speak about this is to tell the world that there is much, much need to reform not only the government but the business sector as well to obey our rules equitably.

I can understand and forgive small businesses, such as sari-sari stores, who might not be so sensitive about their tax duties, but for big businesses and, worst, foreign brands, to be insensitive to our emerging market by shortchanging their tax duties is unforgiveable.

Always do right

In closing, let me say that as one of the nation's senior citizen retirees, my only job now in Solid is to speak to you, our employees, at the beginning of the year to help set the vision for the year to come, and at the end of each year, to review and celebrate the year just passed.

I always look forward to these moments of sharing both bread and thoughts with you, the younger generation, the hope and future of both our company and nation. I always learn so many new things from you and I hope you can still learn a few things from a retiree like me.

The most important thought I would like to share with you today is this: WE SHOULD NEVER, WE WILL NEVER, STOP DOING

WHAT IS RIGHT.

We must always remember what Christ said: "What does it profit a man if he gains the whole world, but loses his soul in the process?" And so, even though most business companies may be tempted to make compromises, to take shortcuts, to achieve profit targets, we will always take the right path, even if by doing so, we achieve less than the sales and profit targets we would have wanted to attain.

While many other companies may be tempted to take the path of smuggling, of tax evasion, to maximize their profits, we will always pay the right taxes on our products, as responsible corporate citizens.

While many others may seek only personal gain, we will always look for ways to share our blessings, especially with the least of our brothers and sisters, especially to support our nation's full development, and all for the ultimate glory of God.

Mabuhay kayo, mabuhay tayo, mabu- hay ang MyPhone at Solid Group, mabuhay ang minamahal nating bansang Pilipinas, at higit sa lahat, mabuhay ang ating Panginoon! (Long live all of you, long live all of us, long live MyPhone and Solid Group, long live our beloved Filipino nation, above all, long live our God!)

XXXX
Tribute to Teachers

World Teachers 'Day Celebration; ULTRA, Pasig City; October 5, 2011

I am honored by your warm welcome and overjoyed to be in the company of men and women who have answered the higher calling of the teaching profession.

I know that teaching must be a vocation that enriches the heart, for certainly no one does it to get enriched in the pocket. Indeed, I know that many of you, for the sake of this vocation, struggle daily with demands of daily needs. But of all the job titles I have had over my many years, the one I carry most proudly is "teacher."

And in many ways, my family and I have entered into a phase of our lives that brings us back to this honorable profession of teaching.

Indeed, we found ourselves becoming teachers in our work of developing Filipino brands like MyPhone and MyHouse.

Teaching though MyPhone

And our lesson plans aimed at removing the colonial mindset of many generations of Filipino consumers and bring back our sense of national pride in our own Filipino brands.

We even developed our own Filipino content which we then offered for free to MyPhone buyers. The content included audio prayers, Filipino history, to *bugtong* (riddles) and *salawikain* (sayings) to give our young customers a chance to see how beautiful being Filipino really is.

We have also had the opportunity to educate by example our friends in industry and government about our values: Honesty in our civic responsibilities including paying the proper taxes and striving to give the best in everything we do, frugality in our lifestyle and the courage to do the right thing no matter what the cost. This is how we do business and this is how we live our lives.

And many times, we have had to pay the cost to do the right thing. We have survived ridicule, obstacles in business, and attacks from evil people and uneven government policies that made it very difficult to do business properly. But we persevered and grew.

Let me tell you our secret - we believe that the Lord has led us to do this therefore we believe that He will sustain and protect us. And so He has.

Sharing through MyHouse

Today, we humbly share some of the fruits the Lord has provided us to honor your chosen teachers for their wonderful achievements. We will be awarding school classrooms built with Modular Insulated Steel Technology. This is a high technology system provided by MyHouse, our newest project that aims to provide modem shelter for schools, businesses and families - "Because we believe the Filipino deserve better!"

We hope that this award to our winning teachers today will motivate them and their students to leam, pursue their dreams but most of all, commit themselves to helping their fellow Filipinos as well, specially the youth.

(NOTE: We committed to build and donate 60 public schoolhouses. To-date, we have already built schoolhouses in areas designated by the Department of Education.)

Lasting lessons

In closing, allow me to share with you the words of two gentlemen, words that deeply impacted into building my years of teaching as among the best lessons in life.

The first was from a Chinese scientist, the genius Mr. Qien Xuesen, the father of China's Nuclear and Space Program. When I met him, I was a very young and shy elementary teacher. He asked me what my vocation was. I said: "I'm just a teacher, sir." He gently admonished me: "Don't be shy about your vocation. You must be very proud of it. In your hands lie the power to mold the minds of the young who will grow to be assets of your county."

I kept this precious lesson for life and shared it not only with my students in my teaching days but to all my co-workers too, in my many business adventures, that we are important in nurturing our colleagues in work striving for good.

The second great man was an Indian philosopher/activist, Mahatma Gandhi. He emphasized that there are Seven Destructive Blunders of the World that cause violence:

1.   Wealth without work
2.   Pleasure without conscience
1.   Knowledge without character
2.   Commerce without morality
3.   Science without humanity
4.   Religion without sacrifice
5.   Politics without principle

In all humility, I would like to add to the great Gandhi's list: "Law without justice." Law without justice is tearing the minds, hearts and souls of all men and women condemned to suffer injustice from laws that too often become a commodity to be twisted, perverted, manipulated by its complexity and incongruity. One thing sure, justice is never speedy. A case can last even after one's lifetime.

As teachers, it is our job to open the minds of our young to these realities, and equip them with the inspiration and skills they need to build a world much better than what we, their elders, have created.

On behalf of a grateful nation, to you, our most beloved and noble teachers, *maraming salamat at mabuhay po kayo!* (thank you and long live!).

IN SUM: MY DEEPEST JOY

I have lived an active and rewarding life, joyfully fulfilling my duties to God, family, business, and country.

At the peak of business operations under my watch, I was responsible for ensuring the sustainability and profitability of several affiliated companies on which
10,0   employees - and their respective families - depended. This meant ensuring the satisfaction of our highly demanding customers, in both local and foreign markets.

Alongside these tasks, I had to nurture the growth of my four children. They became professionals and were not spared their share of heavy work in our companies. In fact, their contributions were invaluable during the 60 years of my entrepreneurial journey until my full retirement in 2005.

By this time, nearly all of my old businesses have come to closure, brought down by the onslaught of globalization and liberalization, as our erstwhile foreign partners took over importation and market- ing of products — after we had introduced and built up their brands in the Philippine market (at great cost to us, in terms of investments, time, effort, and sacrifices).

They left the tedious and hardly profitable task of after-sales servicing to us. Their takeover and subsequent importation of fully- finished goods also forced us to. close down all local manufacturing operations, with the following consequences: Millions of pesos worth of factory equipment ^disposed at fire-sale prices; thousands of workers rendered jobless, at huge additional losses to us as we shouldered all their separation pay and benefits.

Instead of crying over spilt milk, the Lord actually inspired the second generation, my children, to innovate, create, and deliver exciting products, this time enhancing Filipino brands such as MyPhone and MyHouse, delivering great service to ordinary Filipinos, providing high quality and affordable cell phones and houses, covered by full warranties and superior technology.

To date, barely five years in the mobile phone industry, our company has sold over five million units, all fully tax-paid, likewise, hundreds of school houses built in collaboration with the Department of Education. Both products dramatically improving lives.

This is my deepest joy, that my children and grandchildren have stayed true to the course of Entrepreneurship with Honor, maintaining the right quality of being and service to our fellowmen while com- pletely adhering to all the laws of our land, especially in being faithful to the tax duty which our government needs for its smooth governance (no easy shortcuts via corruption and tax evasion).

And I am so thankful to God Almighty for gifting me David, my eldest son, to lead our organization to do honor to Him through good deeds and new products that uplift the lives of many, especially the poor. I am equally grateful to God for Susan, my eldest and only daughter; Jason, my second son, and Vincent, my third and youngest son. I truly appreciate their unqualified support for all the policies, programs and actions of our businesses.

My, oh my! What more can a mother and grandmother ask for? We honor the God of our Land and People by living and building character in service to Him.

AFTERWORD
by Hilarion M, Henares, Jr.
Former Chairman National Economic Council Columnist, Make My Day, Philippine Daily Inquirer

Elena Lim once told a dear friend Pur- ing Tamayo with whom she would like to be alone on a desert island. She said, "Larry Henares, he is amusing, intelligent - and without a single trace of malice in his bones." I am flattered of course, and in turn would certainly relish being on a desert island with Elena Lim whom I once described as a combination of the sexy Mae West, childlike Shirley Temple, and Wonder Woman who gets things done - also, wow, she is a good cook, too, especially her oil-free Chinese lumpia, made of assorted veggies, minced shrimp, pork, and tofu.　　.

I may be amusing and intelligent, but malice? I have been accused of malice in court cases claiming damages that add up to a billion pesos. But I won them all because I wrote satire, defined as "a form of literature directed toward the correction, by means of ridicule, of vice, abuses, inconsistencies, or absurdities in politics, law, religion, education, etc." No malice there, only a desire to correct vice and folly.

I certainly would like to be alone on a desert island with Elena, not only because she is sexy, imbued with childlike wonder, and highly intelligent, but also because she is nationalistic, entrepreneurial, industrious, and with her 50 years experience, will undoubtedly keep me well supplied with food (tiger prawns), a roof over my head (MyHouse Inc.), access to cable TV and Internet (Destiny), television and electronic gadgets (MyPhone, Sony, Samsung, Sanyo, Aiwa), and even a car (Kia and BMW), without my ever lifting a finger to do an ounce of work.

Seriously, Elena Lim is a one of a kind, *sui'generis,* a woman no less, who bom poor, rented out old and worn comic books as a child, worked as a student to earn a law degree, and singlehandedly rose to the topmost ranks of the corporate world - then took on and fought a losing battle against our own colonial-minded government, foreign corporations, the GATT, the WTO and unequal treaties imposed on us by the

United States. If we could clone enough of her kind, we would be the greatest nation on earth.

This book is her voice, and her words. Read and leam.

Profile of Hilarion M. Henares, Jr.

(source: www.philippinefolio.com)

Dr. Hilarion M. Henares, Jr., Doctor of Economics, will probably be known as the Alexander Hamilton of the Philippines. As Hamilton argued for his "Theory of Manufactures" to point the way to the United States' emergence as an industrial power, against Thomas Jefferson's advocacy of a "pastoral economy," so did Henares argue for Philippine Industrialization against American policy to keep the Philippines agricultural.

More than anyone else Henares is the most eloquent spokesman for the Philippine industrial middle class, and he articulated for his generation, the Nationalist Economic Philosophy for the advancement of the common masses. Said Education Secretary Juan Manuel, "Fiercely nationalistic, Henares chose as his field of battle the area of economics. There are many milestones that mark our way to economic emancipation and Henares was there first. He was a visionary, a gadfly, an achiever... who prodded this country almost against its will to accept the challenge of change in the postwar years."

Henares studied in the best schools, Ateneo, University of the Philippines and the Massachusetts Institute of Technology, but his early schooling was in the public schools, where his Senator grandfather put him to prepare him for a political career; he became a cabinet member and a senatorial candidate.

At the age of 30, he was already the head of a multi-million peso business enterprise. Henares became the President of the powerful Philippine Chamber of Industries, and eventually a member of the presidential cabinet as the Chairman of the National Economic Council and Presidential Assistant on Community Development. "One of the most brilliant of my cabinet," said President Diosdado Macapagal, the fifth President of the Philippine Republic.

Henares was at the age of 25, the dean of two graduate schools. He made one movie and it won the Academy Award as fhe Best Documentary of the Year 1957. He sired six children, and was awarded the Presidential Award for Exemplary Family Life by Malacanang in 1960.

He was Young Businessman of the Year 1959 and Industrialist of the Year 1963.

He was a newspaper columnist (front page column "Ways and Means" in pre-martial law Manila Times and in post-Edsa's "Make My Day!" in the Philippine Daily Inquirer, and in the Manila Standard), an essayist, a poet, a TV commentator and a public speaker much in demand.

He was a Presidential Consultant on National Affairs, serving President Fidel V. Ramos, a friend of his youth, who assigned him confidential tasks of national import, and took him along on State Visits; he also served President Gloria Magapagal Arroyo, under whose father Diosdado Macapagal he was the highest paid Cabinet Member. He was an Eisenhower Fellow in the USA, an official guest of Great Britain, Israel, Germany, the People's Republic of China, Indonesia, Soviet Union, and an official representative to conferences abroad.

He is a radio amateur, a computer buff, an electronics expert who makes his own television sets, quadrophonic equipment, electronic organ, and burglar alarms; a photography and movie enthusiast; a gun and book collector. Above all, he is a Nationalist in the great tradition of Claro M. Recto and Jose Rizal, an indefatigable champion of the nationalist cause, whose speeches and writings will show the way and the light for future generations of Filipinos.

The Author

Elena Sen was shaped by war.

She had just turned 12 when the Second World War entered Tacloban, Leyte, her hometown, in 1942.

For three years, the whole country was occupied by the Imperial Army of Japan.

What once was quiet and peaceful country life turned into a nightmare world of daily death, both slow and quick.

For generations bom after the War, there is no way of fully communicating what War means. Life has never been vicarious. Perhaps it accounts for the growing confusion of the Information Age, with its emphasis on virtual reality, on vicarious living and learning.

It is said we are truest at 15, we feel and absorb most then because we still have the courage of innocence, unaware of the perils of absorption.

To survive three years of global war at the age of innocence...

Probably the summation least presumptuous is that the war Elena Sen experienced, coupled with what she had inside her in the first place — wits, guts, humor, diligence, endurance, courage from faith — enabled her to survive and prevail over life's trying risks, threats, and difficulties. Perhaps, after War, all other adversities became smaller.

She once filed a case against several corrupt policemen out to extort money from her. To get the case dropped, they threatened her with all sorts of violence against her person and family. Instead of cowering in fear, she pursued the case harder. She eventually won.

Sony. Samsung. Aiwa. Kia. Petromax. AA Shrimps, Asahi Glass, Starworld Industrial Estate Development, Destiny Cable TV / Internet... These are but some of the brands and businesses she transformed (against tremendous odds) from then unknown names into household words for Filipino families.

The fact that she started out poor — no inheritance, no capital, no connections — makes the accomplishments more formidable.

For the longest time, she was a working student, studying at night, working during the day, with only one pair of shoes and two dresses sewn by her mother. She never developed a taste for soft drinks or imported fruits because she never tasted them while growing up. There was no money for such luxuries. She was already married when she tasted her first apple.

Other highlights:

Bom October 1, 1930, in Tacloban, Leyte, Philippines. Lost her father to illness at three.

Believer in transparency, consistency, and a level playing field in business, simplicity and frugality in lifestyle; above all, putting Christ at the center of life.

Opposed to rapid and destructive liberalization, harmful monopolies, and globalization without humanity, cartels, behest loans, unreasonable policies, overregulation, bureaucratic pettiness, and excessive politics in governance for the interests of a few, whether politicians or powerful, well- connected businessmen.

Has always shown faith in the capability, competence, creativity, and integrity of Filipinos.

Elena Sen Lim. In her own words, a teacher by inclination. Lawyer by circumstance. Entrepreneur by serendipity... and foremost, a common worker who loves her neighbor and serves with values for the glory of her God.

"... Elena has always possessed an uncanny ability to think outside of the box. The exquisite timing of her business ventures have been superb, from the pioneering assembly of SONY television sets to her venture into international shrimp processing and trading to her successful positioning of "MyPhone" in an overcrowded telecommunications market.

"Her fearless attempts to tilt at windmills such as the liberalization of international trade which has placed domestic firms at the mercy of vast, interlocking, well-funded foreign business combines have earned for Elena the admiration and respect of her peers....

"Elena's speeches,.., make excellent reference material for entrepreneurs, economists, business analysts and students of economic history..."
- From the FOREWORD by Senator Sergio R. Osmena III

"*...* I certainly would like to be... with Elena because she... will undoubtedly keep me well supplied with food (tiger prawns), a roof over my head (MyHouse Inc.), cable TV and Internet (Destiny), electronic gadgets (MyPhone, Sony, Samsung, Sanyo, Aiwa), and even a car (Kia and BMW), without my ever lifting a finger...

"Seriously, Elena Lim is one of a kind... a woman no less, who bom poor... singlehandedly rose to the topmost ranks of the corporate world - then took on and fought a losing battle against our own colonial-minded government, foreign corporations, the GATT, the WTO and unequal treaties imposed on us by the United States. If we could clone enough of her kind, we would be the greatest nation on earth.

"This book is her voice, and her words. Read and learn."
- From the AFTERWORD by Hilarion M. Henares, Jr.